# Tarot Spreads

*A Self-Care Guide with Tarot Spreads for Love, Spirituality, Career, and More for Beginners, Including Everything from the Celtic Cross to the Zodiac Spread*

© Copyright 2025 - All rights reserved.

The content contained within this book may not be reproduced, duplicated, or transmitted without direct written permission from the author or the publisher.

Under no circumstances will any blame or legal responsibility be held against the publisher, or author, for any damages, reparation, or monetary loss due to the information contained within this book, either directly or indirectly.

**Legal Notice:**

This book is copyright protected. It is only for personal use. You cannot amend, distribute, sell, use, quote, or paraphrase any part of the content within this book without the consent of the author or publisher.

**Disclaimer Notice:**

Please note the information contained within this document is for educational and entertainment purposes only. All effort has been executed to present accurate, up-to-date, reliable, and complete information. No warranties of any kind are declared or implied. Readers acknowledge that the author is not engaging in the rendering of legal, financial, medical, or professional advice. The content within this book has been derived from various sources. Please consult a licensed professional before attempting any techniques outlined in this book.

By reading this document, the reader agrees that under no circumstances is the author responsible for any losses, direct or indirect, that are incurred as a result of the use of the information contained within this document, including, but not limited to, errors, omissions, or inaccuracies.

# Your Free Gift
# (only available for a limited time)

Thanks for getting this book! If you want to learn more about various spirituality topics, then join Mari Silva's community and get a free guided meditation MP3 for awakening your third eye. This guided meditation mp3 is designed to open and strengthen ones third eye so you can experience a higher state of consciousness. Simply visit the link below the image to get started.

https://spiritualityspot.com/meditation
Or, Scan the QR code!

# Table of Contents

INTRODUCTION ........................................................................................... 1
CHAPTER 1: INTRODUCTION TO TAROT ......................................... 3
CHAPTER 2: THE MAJOR ARCANA .................................................. 12
CHAPTER 3: THE MINOR ARCANA ................................................. 36
CHAPTER 4: CONNECTING WITH THE CARDS ........................... 66
CHAPTER 5: HOW TO READ THE CARDS ..................................... 75
CHAPTER 6: 7 KEY CARD SPREADS ............................................... 85
CHAPTER 7: SPREADS FOR LOVE AND SELF-CARE .................. 96
CHAPTER 8: SPREADS FOR SPIRITUAL DEVELOPMENT .......... 106
CHAPTER 9: SPREADS FOR WORK AND CAREER ..................... 117
CHAPTER 10: CREATE YOUR OWN TAROT SPREADS .............. 127
CONCLUSION ........................................................................................ 134
HERE'S ANOTHER BOOK BY MARI SILVA THAT YOU MIGHT LIKE ..... 137
YOUR FREE GIFT (ONLY AVAILABLE FOR A LIMITED TIME) .................. 138
REFERENCES ........................................................................................ 139
IMAGE SOURCES ................................................................................ 158

# Introduction

Albeit a little more challenging to use than other divination forms, Tarot cards can reveal an immense amount of information about your past, present, and future. It takes time and practice, but using the cards can teach you how to access the information you can use to improve your life. No, they won't reveal your exact future. Most of the information you'll gain already exists in your subconscious; the cards are only a tool you use to access knowledge. However, because Tarot readings rely heavily on intuition, they can also be an excellent form of self-care. By developing your intuition through Tarot readings, you're becoming more aware of your desires and needs. You'll be able to reflect on these and plan your next moves.

You'll your intuition to the cards to achieve all of the above. to achieve all of the above. This book provides thorough guidance on choosing the right deck, which is the first step in working with Tarot cards. You'll be introduced to the most common deck types available today, including the Rider-Waite deck, on which most popular variants are based. The subsequent chapter is a detailed guide on the cards of the Major and Minor Arcanas, which are the two subcategories in each Tarot deck.

Once you've understood the meaning and symbolism of the cards, you'll be ready for a few lessons on tapping into your intuition when working with the cards. Having mastered listening to your gut, you can move on to the following chapters that detail the steps you need to take to read the cards properly. This is a crucial step, as you'll only get accurate answers to your questions if you know how to interpret the messages from the cards. Make sure to refer to the tips and tricks provided in the relevant chapter, as they're designed to make this learning process easier for you.

After learning how to use your intuition to its fullest during the readings, you can move on to the chapters that list all the different spreads you can try. Whether you seek information regarding love, self-care, spiritual development, or work, you'll be able to find the perfect layout for you. Or, you can try some popular spreads that use a specific number. Some of these are suitable particularly for beginners and are great for practicing daily readings. They all come with a practical step-by-step guide, difficulty rating, and tips for modification to ensure your success. Lastly, you'll be encouraged to create your own spreads. You'll receive plenty of practical advice on how to do that. So, if you're ready to delve into the amazing world of Tarot spreads, keep reading.

# Chapter 1: Introduction to Tarot

This first chapter will introduce you to the historical and cultural background of Tarot, including its origins, what it was used for, and how its application has changed through time. It will also look into the most common deck types used today, such as the Rider-Waite, Thoth, and Marseille. You'll also learn about the structure of the cards and the similarities and differences between each.

The earliest reference to tarot cards goes all the way back to the 1440s.[1]

# History of Tarot

The earliest historical reference to Tarot cards originates from 1440s Europe. However, due to the intricate nature of its use at that time, it is believed that Tarot was created a couple of centuries before its European reference. At first, the cards the European artists made were used for games. These decks had 4 suits similar to the Cups, Swords, Discs, and Wands still in use today. Soon after, artists from Venice, Milan, Florence, and Urbino began creating more cards with different illustrations and added them to the decks. These cards were called triumph (trump) cards and were often commissioned by distinguished members of the society. Sometimes the order even dictated that a unique set of cards be created for a noble family featuring members of that family on the trump cards. Since not everyone could afford to hire artists to create customized cards for them, Tarot cards were typically reserved for the privileged until mass printing became available.

By the 18th century, Tarot had spread from Italy to France and gained a new purpose. Users began to attach different meanings to each card, turning it from a fun parlor game to a divinatory tool. According to historical records, Tarot has been used for prophecy from the late 16th century or the early 17th century, albeit in a more simplified way than it's done today. The cards got even more specific meanings a century later, and spreads were created. At the same time, people also learned that Tarot card symbolism is heavily linked to the esoteric teachings of Egyptian religious practices. Some meanings of the Tarot cards have been associated with the ancient lore of the Egyptian gods Osiris and Isis. According to Antoine Court de Gebelin, a French Freemason, the Egyptian teachings made their way to Rome, where the Catholic Church tried (unsuccessfully) to keep them away from the public. While there isn't much historical evidence to support this theory, we know people accepted it. In fact, some of the oldest Tarot decks used today, like the Marseille Tarot, were designed based on Gebelin's theory.

The initial Tarot deck for divination was created in 1791 by French occultist Jean-Baptiste Alliette. He was among the first whose interest in the occult led to the creation of Kabbalah-based art, including Tarot cards linked to hermetic mystics. In the Victorian Era, even upper-class families used Tarot as a parlor game by holding reading séances. A little over a century later, the Rider-Waite Tarot deck was born. Also featuring Kabbalistic symbolism, this deck was the first one with characters to depict the symbolism of the lower cards. Not only were there the customary Swords, Coins, Wands, and Cups, but the creators also used human figures to symbolize the meaning of each card. Due to this, the Original Rider-Waite Tarot deck (also known as the Waite-Smith deck) has become the most widely used deck in history and is still heavily used today.

Since reading methods have evolved since the creation of the first Tarot cards, they are now available in a broad range of designs. And more importantly, Tarot is known and accessible to anyone who wants to learn how to use them for divinatory, spiritual, and many other purposes. And while the cards themselves haven't changed much, the intricate nature of their use made it possible for readers to add their own spin to the traditional meanings of a layout.

## Tarot Decks Used Today

Several different Tarot decks are in use today, each with its own theme and symbolism. Here are some of the most popular ones.

### Rider-Waite

The Rider-Waite suit was assembled by Arthur Edward White and illustrated by Pamela Coleman Smith in 1909. It has similar interpretations of the Major Arcana and Minor Arcana cards as its classical predecessor did in the 18th and 19th centuries. However, its illustration is much more colorful, giving way to vibrant imagery, which users often find helpful for intuitive readings. Due to their classical imagery, most people find learning how to use these cards pretty straightforward. The images have origins in Paganism, beliefs that existed in the medieval eras, and even Christianity. You'll learn more about the symbolism of the Rider-Waite cards later in the book.

### Thoth

Aleister Crowley – a famous English occultist and rival of White – designed another set of cards, the Thoth deck. The cards in this deck were painted by Frieda Harries and depicted a slightly different symbolism for Tarot cards. Crowley and Harries got ideas for the card imagery from several spiritual systems, the occult, and Crowley's own unique spiritual views.

When compared to the Rider-Waite deck, the Thoth deck shows several distinctive differences. Moving away from intuitive imagery, Crowley opted for less-classical design. For example, the Fool card in the

Thoth deck is depicted as the Green Man, the universal symbol of life, birth, and rebirth. Meanwhile, this card portrays a young man facing a life-changing journey in the Rider-Waite deck. This and similar changes give readers a fresh perspective on the classical Tarot card symbolism and conjure new ideas and messages when reading the cards.

Crowley also changed the names of some of the cards. For example, the Strength card in the Major Arcana is called Naked Lust in the Thoth. The Pentacles are named *Discs*, and the numerical and astrological correspondences of several cards have changed. These features allow readers to interpret the cards in a new and unique way.

### Marseille

One of the oldest Tarot decks still used today is the Marseille deck. The Marseille deck is a true classic created by François Gassman in Geneva, Switzerland. Despite featuring the same Major Arcana and Minor Arcana cards as many contemporary decks, this one has traditional baroque-style imagery. It has several variations, but most cards have kept their primary French names. Not only that, but when it comes to the four suits, the creator stayed true to the original naming traditions, leaving them as Cups (Coupes), Swords (Épées), Coins (Deniers), and Clubs (Bâtons).

## The Cards

Most Tarot decks (Rider-Waite, Thoth, and Marseille) have 78 cards, although some artists can create one or two unique additions to the standard pack, making decks with 79 or 80 cards. Each card has its own symbolism and meaning, which can be used in single-card readings. However, when reading spreads, the meaning of the cards can differ, depending on their combination in the layout. The cards are divided into two categories based on their meanings and symbolism. These categories include the Major Arcana (22 cards depicting a journey, also known as the bigger picture showing the answer you're seeking) and the Minor Arcana (56 cards revealing the minor nuances affecting the answer).

Not only do different Tarot decks have different names (after the artists that created them), but the cards in these decks can have names and several symbols that vary greatly depending on the deck's purpose. Some cards have numbers (in Roman numerals) and names, while others will have only one of the two. Either way, having a name and/or number helps familiarize new readers with cards and their meanings. The number of cards typically stays the same (78). However, the artists might change the order of their numbering to represent a slightly different theme. Other artists will only provide symbolic images to the cards in their deck without naming or numbering them. These are typically used by those who prefer to rely on intuitive readings and not traditional card meanings.

## The Best Deck for Beginners

Being the first mass-distributed Tarot decks in history, the original Rider-Waite deck is the most widely researched one that you can find. Because there is no shortage of information about the symbolism and use of this deck, it's the most recommended Tarot deck for beginners. The standard description makes it easy to familiarize yourself with the essential functions and incorporate them into your daily practices. As one of the most popular versions of the original Rider-Waite tarot deck, the Radiant Rider-Waite deck is also recommended to beginners due to its similarity with its predecessor. If you find these too esoteric, you can always try your luck with the Classical Tarot. This deck captures symbols you can interpret intuitively, which many find easier.

## How to Choose the Right Tarot Deck

Most Tarot decks you'll find today are Rider-Waite derivatives, which is why this book will focus only on this deck. You're free to choose whichever Tarot decks you wish to work with. Below are some tips on finding the right deck for beginners.

### Look for Intuitive Connections with the Cards

The best way to find the right deck is to choose the one you are drawn to. While you can get recommendations for specific decks, you should never go by other people's experiences. Look at the recommended decks, but if you don't feel a personal connection to them, it means that they simply aren't suitable for you and your personality. However, if your gut tells you to learn more about a deck (or certain cards in the deck), you should explore them more deeply. Because of this, it's always better to buy your first Tarot deck in person. Feel free to touch the cards and contemplate the type of energy you pick up from them. You should feel a personal connection with at least one or more cards in the deck. Whether you're getting it from a bookstore or a new-age shop, you'll get a much better picture of your reaction to the cards than if you were to buy them online. That said, if your only option for buying a Tarot deck is purchasing them online, explore the cards they contain beforehand. A quick Google search of the deck you're considering should provide you with enough imagery to decide whether you can connect to the cards.

**Explore the Imagery of the Cards**

Even if you're buying them in a store, doing a little research on the imagery of the cards is always a good idea. Make sure to go through the cards individually, stopping at each to check your response to them. You'll have a different reaction to the decks. For example, some people are drawn to intricate patterns, while others like vivid colors. Some people can't take their eyes off the images, while others will pick up on specific pieces of the artwork. You should also check different variations of the same deck to see if your reaction is the same to all of them. For example, some feel a much stronger connection to the Radiant Rider-Waite deck than to the traditional Rider-Waite deck simply because it uses more vivid imagery.

While exploring, you should look at the meaning of the cards too. If you can pick up the essence of the cards intuitively, it's a sure sign that you've found the right deck. Look at all the Major Arcana and Minor Arcana cards to see if you find most of them visually appealing. Some decks have significant differences in the illustrations, and some readers find non-traditional depictions extremely unappealing.

**Consider Your Experience Level**

Beginners often prefer learning the basics of Tarot with straightforward symbolism, like the one used on the Rider-Waite deck. Others like a more minimalist design and will choose the likes of the Everyday Tarot Deck, which allows a more practical approach to connecting with the imagery. On the other hand, those with some experience with Tarot prefer more challenging and complex decks, like the Thoth deck. Make sure to match your experience level with your connection with the cards. Whether you find it easier to work with the classical Rider-Waite deck becomes irrelevant if you can't form an intuitive link with them.

**Determine if You Want a Traditional or Modern Deck**

Some people are instinctively drawn to contemporary imagery, often created by independent artists with a unique view of Tarot symbols. They find these more relevant to our times and come in handy for resolving modern issues. Others are intrigued by the classical decks like the Marseille and the Rider-Waite deck, with their fascinating, European-style imagery. These are better suited for answering age-old questions and looking at the bigger picture in every situation. That said, if you feel a stronger connection with a contemporary design, you can still use them to reveal more in-depth information about the outcome you're interested in exploring. You'll just need to listen to your intuition, and you'll be able to work with any deck.

### Check Out the Literature

Most Tarot card artists include a booklet explaining the meaning of the cards in the deck they've created. You can also learn about the cards' symbolism and other helpful information from this small guide. If the deck you've purchased or are about to buy doesn't come with a complementary guide or the latter lacks the information you're looking for, don't worry; you can still learn about the cards (including whether you'll be able to work with them) by looking them up online. Look for reviews from other users, guides on them, or e-books explaining how to work with the particular deck. On the other hand, if you prefer to rely solely on your gut, you can find the lack of predefined symbolism refreshing. Not having preconceived notions about the cards encourages you to hone your intuition even more.

### Find the Right Size

Tarot cards come in many sizes; you can pick the one that best fits your needs and purposes. For example, if you do small daily rituals to practice your craft but travel a lot, you should choose mini Tarot cards. These fit perfectly into any bag, so you can take them anywhere. If you prefer to do readings in the privacy of your home, any regular-sized deck will work as long as you can bond with its energy. On the other hand, if you plan to do group readings with family or friends, you'll find giant Tarot decks handy. Ensure you're getting the size you and whoever else will be using the cards are comfortable handling when shuffling and making the spread.

### Consider How You Want to Use the Tarot Cards

The purpose of the Tarot cards will also have a bearing on your decision. Some decks are better suited for answering questions about finding peace and harmony in your life. Others are better for intuitive readings or connecting to your spiritual desires. If your practice includes earth-based rituals and spells, choose a deck that accommodates this. There are Tarot decks with versatile backgrounds and symbolism that can accommodate a range of purposes. If you have several uses for your cards, get one that fits all your needs and desires. Experienced readers have several decks on hand. However, for beginners, it's recommended to have only one to learn the basics and develop your intuition enough for it to connect to the cards at all times.

### Pay Attention to Quality

The quality of the cards also matters as you'll need something you can use for years and possibly daily. Unfortunately, many inexpensive decks are not quality cards and will tear or get damaged only after a few uses. If you plan to use your cards regularly, investing a little more in a good-quality deck is better than buying something that will fall apart after a couple of uses.

### Buy Your Tarot Cards

Some still believe that Tarot cards should only be gifted and not bought by oneself, but this deprives you of the opportunity to check if you'll have a connection with them. No matter how good the gifter's intentions were when they purchased the deck for you, if you can't connect to the cards, you'll have no use for them. Of course, if you have a close friend or a loved one whom you can hint about the deck to which you feel drawn, feel free to do so.

## The Benefits of Practicing Tarot Reading

Practicing Tarot reading has many benefits, regardless of which decks you use. Some of these benefits are listed below.

### You'll Gain Clarity in Life

Tarot card readings are great for gaining insight into different life situations. Getting clarity on some difficult matters can help you make the next step. The cards also give you a fresh perspective on concerns you mistakenly believed resolved but which were stopping you from reaching your full potential.

### You Can Focus on Improving Certain Areas of Life

Tarot cards can also give a better understanding of your personality. For example, if you have a trait that negatively impacts your ability to grow personally, the cards can highlight it. Once you've been made aware of the negative quality, you can start improving it. Remember, no matter how prosperous your life is, there is always room for self-improvement. Tarot cards are the ideal tools for picking up the areas that you still need to work on.

### You Can Find Peace and Harmony

Sometimes, your own negativity will hold you back the most, and the cards can point this out. They can also highlight the positive aspects of life you should focus on instead of obsessing over the negative experiences. This can give you the peace of mind you need, alleviating anxiety and creating harmony between the different aspects of your life.

### You'll Make Better Decisions

If you're at a crossroads in life and have trouble deciding how to move forward, consulting the Tarot cards can help you make the right decision. The cards will not predict the exact future or tell you how to make decisions. However, they will give you the necessary insight to make the best decision.

### You Can Make Improvements to Your Life

If you're looking to transform your life, Tarot card reading is a perfect way to do this. The cards can highlight new talents you can nurture, skills to discover and hone, and any aspects of your personality you need to focus on to become a better version of yourself.

### You Can Nurture Your Relationships

Because they help you replace negative influences with positive ones, Tarot cards often prompt people to take a risk they wouldn't otherwise take. One of the greatest (and most rewarding) risks you can take is to open yourself up in your relationships. Tarot readings can give the reassurance you need when taking risks to establish a loving and harmonious relationship with your loved ones. Having created these, you'll become much happier, enabling you to appreciate the positive aspects even more and inspiring you to work on the negative ones.

# Chapter 2: The Major Arcana

The Rider-Waite tarot deck is split into two sub-groups, The Major Arcana and The Minor Arcana. Each soul is on a journey to learn lessons and reach enlightenment. The Major Arcana cards, also called The Trump cards, represent the archetypal themes and karmic influences that affect your journey. Each card holds a beautiful, deep, and complex meaning, but this is part of what makes them fascinating. Understanding these cards will give you the keys to uncovering your consciousness and learning all life's lessons.

The Major Arcana.[9]

There are twenty-one numbered Major Arcana cards and one unnumbered which is called "The Fool card." The Fool is the most significant card and the star of the story. He takes a life-altering journey through all the Major Arcana cards. He meets different characters along the way, and each one has a lesson to teach him until he finishes his journey in the last card, "The World card." The only way to understand the Major Arcana cards is to explore and learn about the *Fool's journey.*

# The Fool's Journey
# The Fool

**Number**
Zero

**Element**
Air

**Corresponding Planet**
Uranus

**Zodiac Sign**
Aquarius

**Upright Meaning (if the card appears upright, not upside-down)**

Free spirit, spontaneity, innocence, new beginnings, adventure, faith, freedom, eccentricity, impulsiveness, purity, originality, and courage.

The Fool upward card represents new opportunities and beginnings. Like the

The fool.'

Fool, you are embarking on a new journey into the unknown. You don't need a destination; you are following your heart and committing to the path. It can seem like a crazy or risky adventure, but you take a leap of faith and trust that the Universe will guide you. The Fool will encourage you to open your heart and mind to what's coming. Let go of your worries and fear and step into the unknown. Whatever happens, happens, you're not the one in control, but you have faith in the Universe's plan for you. You are experiencing a new world where you will learn new lessons and grow.

**Reversed Meanings (if the card appears upside-down)**

Lacking adventure, stupidity, restrictions, not thinking things through, playing it safe, chaos, naivety, lack of direction, being gullible, and poor judgment.

The Fool reversed means that you have a new project or idea but aren't ready to share it with the world. You don't have faith in yourself and are questioning your abilities, or you feel that this isn't the right time. Something is standing in your way, and you allow it to hold you back from reaching your full potential. You choose to wait because you are afraid to take a risk. You are standing still, refusing to take any new steps. However, if you have been reckless recently, the reverse Fool card reminds you to slow down and consider the consequences of your actions.

The story begins with the Fool feeling inspired and excited as he embarks on his new journey. However, there is so much that he still needs to learn. He is naive as this is his first adventure, so he is unaware that he is about to walk off a cliff. Yet, he is very enthusiastic, and his heart is in the right place. He is extremely hopeful and feels that anything is possible. He takes a moment and prepares himself to get into a different mindset than his own, the mindset of the Magician.

# The Magician

The magician.[4]

**Number**
One
**Element**
Air
**Corresponding Planet**
Mercury
**Zodiac Sign**
Gemini
**Upright Meaning**

Creativity, visualization, action, manifesting desire, power, willpower, smooth-talking, inspiration, skill, self-employment, resourcefulness, and communication.

The upward Magician card represents magic, transformation, healing, and willpower. He uses the power of the elements to inspire a strong will and a desire for change in the fool. He is the link between above and below or heaven and Earth. The Magician understands that the world and the human mind aren't different from one another. In fact, one is a reflection of the other. This means that if one uses their inner power, they can create a beautiful world inside of them which will reflect on their external world. The Magician inspires you to dig deep and reach your full potential. Whether it's a new relationship, a job, or a career, it pushes you to act now and make the necessary changes. Some opportunities come once in a lifetime; if you miss them, there is no going back.

**Reversed Meaning**

Bad intentions, deceit, manipulation, lying, feeling out of your depth, poor communication skills, creativity block, and abuse of power.

The reversed Magician card means that you aren't tapping into your creativity. Maybe you feel that the world isn't ready for your ideas, or you don't have the confidence to share your creativity with others. It can also mean that you lack leadership skills.

As the Fool goes into the Magician's mindset, he harnesses his inner power to make his dreams come true. He believes in the power of magic and that he can perform miracles if he works with the universe. While the fool is discovering his metaphysical gifts, he encounters the High Priestess.

## The High Priestess

**Number**

Two

**Element**

Water

**Corresponding Planet**

The Moon

**Zodiac Sign**

Cancer

**Upright Meaning**

Divine femininity, mystery, inner voice, sensuality, intuition, desire, high power, unattainability, thirst for knowledge, fertility, subconscious, mind, and creativity.

The high priestess.⁵

The High Priestess's upright card signifies that you should trust your instincts and make the right choices for yourself. Listen to your gut and ignore what everyone tells you. The Universe is on your side, helping you and sending you signs. It is working with you to achieve your dreams. The card can also mean that the knowledge you seek is deep inside you. Your inner divine female is ready to guide you and give you the answers you seek. The High Priestess encourages you to accomplish anything you set your mind to and provides you with answers. She wants you to protect your heart and mind from negative thoughts and better understand your abilities and skills so you can go far in life.

**Reversed Meaning**

Silence, secrets, sexual tension, poor psychic abilities, superficiality, fertility issues, hidden motives, angry outbursts, confusion, repressed intuition, withdrawal, and unwanted attention.

The card suggests that although looking inward will grant you the wisdom you seek, you will struggle with indecisiveness and a wandering mind. You will ignore your goals and dreams and focus on your drama. It can also mean that no one really knows you as you don't share your true self with the world. You lack self-confidence and constantly question yourself. You also live in denial and aren't aware of your inner abilities. Your glass is half empty as you are focused on the negative things in life.

The Fool meets the High Priestess as he prepares to expand his powers and develops a better understanding of the spiritual and physical worlds. She stands as a guard to the human's intuition and invites the Fool to join her in a world of Divine wisdom and knowledge. She becomes his teacher.

The fool wonders if he is in the right direction, and this is when his mother, The Empress, appears.

# The Empress

**Number**
Three

**Element**
Fire

**Corresponding Planet**
Venus

**Zodiac Sign**
Taurus

**Upright Meaning**
Fertility, nurturing, femininity, abundance, sensuality, safety, divine figure, security, beauty, creation, peacefulness, motherhood, harmony, pregnancy, success, and connection with nature.

The empress.⁶

The Empress represents connecting with your feminine side, which includes nurturing, sensuality, elegance, and fertility. Connecting with your femininity is necessary as it creates a balance between men and women and invites beauty into your life. The Empress urges you to connect with your five senses and experience all life's pleasures through them. Tap into your creative mind and express yourself through art or music. She wants to show you that you are growing and are about to achieve all your dreams. The Empress reminds you to be grateful because you have everything you need to be happy.

**Reversed Meaning**

Smothering, insecurity, inability to move forward, infertility, lack of progress, negligence, low self-confidence, and disharmony.

The reversed Empress card reminds you to take care of yourself because you have been ignoring your needs for so long. You have been focusing on people's feelings and neglecting your own. You give others power and let them influence your actions and decisions. The reversed Empress wants to show you that giving your time and effort to others is affecting your well-being. The card can also mean you are experiencing a creativity block and need to connect with nature.

The Empress represents nurturing and fertility and reminds the fool to connect with Mother Nature. Then his father, The Emperor, appears.

# The Emperor

**Number**
Four

**Element**
Fire

**Corresponding Planet**
Mars

**Zodiac Sign**
Aries

**Upright Meaning**
Leadership, stability, logic, structure, practicality, protection, providing, authority, safety, dependability, maturity, and fatherhood.

The emperor.'

This card is a symbol of a father figure. Whether you are a man or woman, it represents your role as a protector and provider of your family. You bring stability to your loved ones; they depend on you and see you as a role model. The Emperor reflects your position and the respect that comes with it. You are a leader who desires power; you know what you want and are prepared to go after it. As a leader, you are firm but fair and always open to hearing others' input, but you end up doing what you believe is right.

**Reversed Meaning**

Tyranny, abuse of power, domineering, controlling, father issues, overbearing, lack of control, overpowering, stubbornness, and manipulative.

The Reversed Emperor reminds you that you are abusing your power and can be too controlling. The card invites you to assess your leadership style, look within yourself, and evaluate how you treat others.

When The Emperor meets the Fool, he provides him with specific rules that he must follow to guarantee that his journey is safe and prosperous. The Emperor reminds the Fool that he should carry his traditions in his heart because they will keep him level-headed and grounded as he experiences a spiritual awakening. The Fool wants to explore spirituality and hopes to find an experienced teacher to guide him. This is when The Hierophant appears.

# The Hierophant

**Number**
Five

**Element**
Earth

**Corresponding Planet**
Venus

**Zodiac Sign**
Taurus

**Upright Meaning**

Teamwork, religion, safety, belief, education, commitment, spiritual wisdom, traditions, marriage, conformity, and sharing knowledge.

This card reminds you to embrace traditional ideas and thoughts. Even when you are tempted to experience the unconventional parts of life, set some boundaries so you don't compromise your beliefs. It also means that you are a follower, not a leader, and prefer to stay with the conventional rather than try something new.

The hierophant.⁸

**Reversed Meaning**

Peer pressure, freedom, non-conformity, personal belief, rebellion, challenging traditions, new methods, and ignorance.

The reversed Hierophant tarot represents rebelling and breaking the rules. It invites you to let go of the old rules that have been governing your life. Challenge social norms and ask yourself if they are worth following or not.

The Hierophant influences the Fool to learn the traditions and beliefs of his culture and conform to social norms.

Now the Fool begins to experience loneliness and yearns for a sexual partnership and hopes to find his soulmate and experience The Lovers.

# The Lovers

**Number**

Six

**Element**

Air

**Corresponding Planet**

Mercury

**Zodiac Sign**

Gemini

The lovers.'

**Upright Meaning**

Soulmates, relationships, love, sexual bonds, passion, connection, and physical attraction.

This card represents the union and harmony between a couple. When you meet your soulmate, what you feel is beyond physical attraction; it is a divine feeling that only true lovers experience. It is a pure relationship built on trust, closeness, and honesty.

**Reverse Meaning**

Impulsive choices, trust issues, conflicts, lack of intimacy, broken promises, detachment, and coldness.

The reversed Lovers card represents challenges in a relationship. You and your partner are unable to communicate, and the time has come to go your separate ways.

The Lovers teach the Fool cooperation and balance his feminine and masculine sides. Now, he feels that he has learned enough to succeed in life, so he rides The Chariot to take a journey to achieve his goals.

# The Chariot

**Number**
Seven

**Element**
Water

**Corresponding Planet**
The Moon

**Zodiac Sign**
Cancer

**Upward Meaning**

Action, direction, strength, control, ambition, tenacity, determination, motivation, and success.

This card means you are ready to apply what you have learned, make the right decisions, and take action. The Chariot encourages you to harness your inner power to achieve the goals you have set for yourself.

The chariot.[10]

**Reversed Meaning**

Hostility, lack of direction, helplessness, and loss of control.

The Chariot reversed tells you you need to change your plan or direction because whatever project or task you are working on won't help you achieve your goals. If you are working on something and feel stuck, assess the situation, and consider changing directions.

The Fool has acquired Strength through his journey that tames the fiery ambition he experienced on The Chariot. He now understands that some goals take longer to achieve, which leads him to experience maturity and growth.

# The Strength

**Number**
Eight

**Element**
Fire

**Corresponding Planet**
The Sun

**Zodiac Sign**
Leo

**Upright Meaning**
Courage, health, bravery, inner power, boldness, kindness, and compassion.

This card symbolizes the inner strength that drives you to overcome any challenges you face. You are calm, patient, mature, and composed. You have a quiet presence that influences those around you. You have the courage to achieve anything, even if you are afraid.

Strength.[11]

**Reversed Meaning**
Self-doubt, disbelief, vulnerability, weakness, insecurity, anxiety, and low self-esteem.

This card means that you are experiencing setbacks and losing your confidence. Tap into your inner strength and let it empower you.

The Fool needs to reflect on everything he has learned so far, so he spends some time by himself and becomes The Hermit. As The Hermit, he tries to make sense of the world. This leads him to discover that there are no coincidences and everything is going according to the Universe's plan.

# The Hermit

**Number**
Nine

**Element**
Earth

**Corresponding Planet**
Mercury

**Zodiac Sign**
Virgo

**Upright Meaning**

Guidance, contemplation, meditation, self-discovery, retreat, introspection, and solitude.

This card represents taking a break from your social life and spending time alone to focus on your inner self. Search deep into your soul to find that the truth and knowledge you seek are within you.

The hermit.[18]

**Reversed Meaning**

Withdrawal, seclusion, loneliness, restriction, rejection, paranoia, and isolation.

This card has two meanings: either you are too focused on your inner self or not at all. It reminds you to spend some time nurturing your spiritual side by meditating and rebuilding yourself. However, if you spend too much time on self-reflection, this card suggests that you have isolated yourself and become a hermit. Remember the value of personal relationships and connecting with others.

The Fool is introduced to The Wheel of Fortune, where he learns about the concept of Fate. Everything happens for a reason and at the right time.

# The Wheel of Fortune

**Number**

Ten

**Element**

Fire

**Corresponding Planet**

Jupiter

**Zodiac Sign**

Capricorn

Wheel of fortune.[18]

**Upright Meaning**

Chance, good luck, the cycle of life, destiny, decisive moments, karma, and soulmates.

This card reminds you that life is constantly moving and changing. No matter how bad things are now, they will get better. You will experience good fortune sooner or later. However, if things are going well, this can also change. Life is an ongoing cycle, so enjoy what you have now because you don't know what the future will bring,

**Reversed Meaning**

Setbacks, bad luck, delays, disorder, disruptions, and unwelcome change.

This reversed card indicates bad luck. You will find your life changing for the worst, and you can do nothing to fix it. However, taking responsibility for your actions and believing you are in control can change your destiny.

The Fool then learns that there is justice and consequences for his actions.

# Justice

Justice.¹⁴

**Number**
Eleven

**Element**
Air

**Corresponding Planet**
Venus

**Zodiac Sign**
Libra

**Upright Meaning**

Justice, law, karma, consequences, truth, fairness, and honesty.

This card reminds you that you will pay the price for your actions. If you live an honest life without harming others, you are safe. However, you will be held accountable for your mistakes if you haven't.

**Reversed Meaning**

Injustice, dishonesty, corruption, and lack of responsibility.

This card means you made a mistake but are afraid to admit it. So, you either keep it hidden or confess and make things right. It also means you refuse to take responsibility for your mistakes and blame others for them.

The Fool now becomes The Hanged Man and sets out to discover the world.

# The Hanged Man

**Number**

Twelve

**Element**

Earth

**Corresponding Planet**

Venus

**Zodiac Sign**

Taurus

**Upright Meaning**

Letting go, giving up, sacrificing, thoughts, waiting, and perspective.

This card wants you to let go of your old way of thinking, change your perspective, and see the world differently. The appearance of this card in a reading means that the projects you are working on will suddenly stop. Take this time to reassess your direction. The Universe has paused your projects because something better is coming along.

The hanged man.[15]

**Reversed Meaning**

Delays, indecision, stagnation, resistance, apathy, and avoidance.

This card means you are keeping yourself busy because you don't want to confront your issues. Your mind and body want you to slow down and pay attention to them.

The Fool now experiences Death as his old self fades away, and he is a new man embarking on the next chapter in his life.

# Death

**Number**
Thirteen

**Element**
Water

**Corresponding Planet**
Pluto

**Zodiac Sign**
Scorpio

**Upright Meaning**

Release, transformation, letting go, endings, and transitions.

The Death card doesn't hold a negative meaning. It represents letting go of a life that no longer serves you and freeing space for something that will add value and meaning to your life. Release the past and welcome new opportunities. Transformation allows you to let go of the old and welcome the new.

Death.[16]

**Reversed Meaning**

Decay, fear of change, and stagnation.

Reversed Death card indicates that you are resisting change. You still hold on to old perspectives that no longer serve you. As a result, you feel stuck and experience periods of stagnation.

Now, as the Fool lets go of the past, he is at peace. He is much wiser and more patient as he is able to find balance with Temperance. He understands that not everything needs to happen right away.

# Temperance

**Number**
Fourteen

**Element**
Fire

**Corresponding Planet**
Jupiter

**Zodiac Sign**
Sagittarius

**Upward Meaning**
Balance, serenity, harmony, peace, tranquility, patience, and moderation.

This card reminds you to stay calm, especially when life is getting hectic or stressful. Remain level-headed and in control of your emotions, and don't allow anything to ruin your day. It invites you to welcome people with different perspectives and accept them instead of being stubborn.

Temperance.[17]

**Reversed Meaning**
Imbalance, hastiness, recklessness, excess, and discord.

This card reminds you to let go of excess and embrace moderation. It also indicates that things aren't going right for you. Assess your life, make the necessary adjustments, and bring back the flow.

The Fool tries to move forward, but he is still stuck in the past and unable to let go. The Devil shows up and encourages him to look at the parts of his past that prevent him from moving forward.

# The Devil

**Number**
Fifteen

**Element**
Earth

**Corresponding Planet**
Saturn

**Zodiac Sign**
Capricorn

**Upward Meaning**

Obsession, secrecy, adultery, dependency, and mental illness.

This card shows your dark side and the negativity within you that prevents you from growing. Whether it's a toxic relationship, addiction, or negative thoughts, you feel trapped. You choose instant gratification over your well-being and long-term goals.

The devil.[18]

**Reversed Meaning**

Detachment, realization, independence, revelation, and regaining control.

This card appears when you are about to make a discovery. But you are held back by your unhealthy lifestyle or attachments. You must let go of your darkness before embracing a new and better version of yourself.

The Fool gets help from The Tower by forcing him to let go of the shackles of the past. Although this can feel scary, it's for his own good and can free him.

# The Tower

**Number**
Sixteen

**Element**
Fire

**Corresponding Planet**
Mars

**Zodiac Sign**
Aries

The tower.[19]

**Upright Meaning**

Disaster, chaos, destruction, and trauma.

When this card appears, expect your life to take a turn for the worse. Chaos and destruction will bring a great change into your life. This can be a health issue, divorce, financial troubles, losing your job, or the death of a loved one.

**Reversed Meaning**

Averting distance, resisting change, and delaying the inevitable.

This also indicates change, but unlike the upright Tower where things are beyond your control, you are the one making the changes. You are questioning everything, like your purpose and life's meaning, which will lead you to experience a spiritual awakening.

The Star shows up to light his way, guides him, and gives him hope. The Fool feels its inspiration as he shows his truest self.

# The Star

**Number**
Seventeen

**Element**
Air

**Corresponding Planet**
Uranus

**Zodiac Sign**
Aquarius

**Upright Meaning**

Hope, positivity, inspiration, healing, creativity, and renewal.

The star.[30]

The Star brings hope after the destruction caused by The Tower. After everything you have been through, you now know who you truly are. You are one with the universe and can handle anything life throws at you. This is a new chapter where you will experience peace and mental stability.

**Reversed Meaning**

Despair, boredom, negativity, and hopelessness.

This indicates that you have stopped believing in your connection with the universe. You feel the Divine isn't on your side and are questioning everything happening to you, "Why is this happening to me?"

The Moon represents the Fool's fears that interfere with his peace of mind. His old anxieties and the things he put behind him are returning to haunt him.

# The Moon

**Number**
Eighteen

**Element**
Water

**Corresponding Planet**
Neptune

**Zodiac Sign**
Pisces

**Upright Meaning**
Deception, confusion, fear, and insecurity.

This card represents letting your fear interfere with your present and future. This can be the result of suppressing your emotions and not dealing with them. It also indicates a state of illusion, so refrain from making decisions when this card appears.

**Reversed Meaning**
Insomnia, bad dress, and unhappiness.

The reversed Moon means that you understand the impact of your fears and anxieties on your life and the steps you need to take to make the necessary changes.

Now the Fool has overcome his anxieties and fears and has transformed into The Sun. He has become a new man -aware of his purpose in life. He is sharing his truest self with the world and is guiding others to do the same.

The moon.[21]

# The Sun

**Number**
Nineteen

**Element**
Fire

**Corresponding Planet**
The Sun

**Zodiac Sign**
Leo

**Upright Meaning**
Enlightenment, vitality, joy, marriage, and success.

The Sun reminds you of your positivity and optimism. People enjoy your warm personality and ability to see the silver lining in everything. Your sunny attitude will give you the strength to handle whatever comes your way. The Sun also reminds you that things will always get better.

The sun.²³

**Reversed Meaning**
Lack of clarity, sadness, and false impressions.

This card is saying that you have been taking life seriously, and it's time to reach into your inner child and have fun. It is OK to take a break every once in a while and to enjoy yourself. The card also reminds you to look on the bright side.

The Fool is now aware of his true purpose and knows his destiny. Everything is real. There are no lies or illusions left, similar to a final Judgment.

# Judgment

**Number**
Twenty

**Element**
Fire

**Corresponding Planet**
Pluto

**Zodiac Sign**
None

**Upright Meaning**

Awakening, transition, renewal, and redemption.

This card means that you are finally aware of your purpose in life. You are answering your spiritual calling as you shed your old self and embrace the real you. This card appears when everything in your life has fallen into place and you are ready to enter a significant chapter in your life.

Judgment.[28]

**Reversed Meaning**

Poor decisions, self-doubt, and stagnation.

Pay attention if you see this card because the Universe is sending you a message. Something big is about to happen in your life, but you aren't hearing the Universe's call or seeing the signs.

The Fool has completed his journey and has grasped everything The World is trying to teach him. He has learned many lessons and is celebrating his accomplishments.

# The World

**Number**

Twenty-One

**Element**

Earth

**Corresponding Planet**

Saturn

**Zodiac Sign**

None

**Upright Meaning**

Achievement, success, possibility, and fulfillment.

The world."

If you see the World card, you should be proud of yourself. You have achieved one of your biggest goals and are reveling in your success, like getting a promotion, marrying your soulmate, having a child, or graduating college. You have made your dream a reality. Take a moment to reflect on your journey and the lessons you have learned, and be grateful for everything you have accomplished.

**Reversed Meaning**

Failed plans, stagnation, and delayed success.

This card indicates your desire for closure. You have to accept that things have changed so you can move on from the past. It can also mean you want to achieve a big goal and aren't prepared for it.

The Fool's journey mirrors each person's path in life. You begin it naive and inexperienced but learn through experiences and taking risks. Life is the best teacher one can ask for; just pay attention to what it's trying to teach you.

# Chapter 3: The Minor Arcana

The Minor Arcana tarot is the second subgroup of cards in the Rider-Waite tarot deck. There are fifty-six cards, each symbolizing the adversity and affliction of the human experience. Although these cards are referred to as "minor," they are no less significant or influential than the Major Arcana cards. They provide you with insight into your day-to-day life and shed light on the changes you need to make to achieve your goals.

Minor arcana.[25]

Unlike the Major Arcana cards that focus on your longer-term experiences, the Minor Arcana have a temporary impact as they represent what goes on in your life in the present moment. The Minor Arcana Cards are categorized into four different suits.

1. Cups
2. Swords
3. Pentacles
4. Wands

Each consists of ten numbered cards and four court cards: the King, Queen, Knight, and Page. Each suit focuses on various parts of your life.

## The Suit of Cups

**Keywords**

Intuition, emotions, relationships, and feelings.

**Element**

Water

**Alternative Names**

Chalices, goblets, or vessels.

**Jungian Function**

Feeling

The Suit of Cups represents your emotions, feelings, and the daily energy that flows inside you. It shows your behavior and interactions with the people in your life. These cards also reflect how you connect with yourself and your loved ones. When the suit of Cup cards is strong, they symbolize your compassionate, kind-hearted, caring, creative, and empathetic nature. You can put yourself in other people's shoes and relate to them. It also means that you are extremely intuitive, and some call you psychic.

When these cards are weak, you live in a fantasy world, and you don't listen to reason or facts.

## Ace of Suits

**Element**

Water

**Corresponding Planet**

Mercury

**Zodiac Sign**

Capricorn

**Upright Meaning**

Happiness, creativity, new beginnings, relationships, fulfillment, love, pregnancy, new connections, fertility, socializing, joy, and festivities.

**Reversed Meaning**

End of relationships, self-love, anguish, repressed emotions, bad news, intuition, infertility, unrequited love, miscarriages, breakups, and sadness.

## Two of Cups

**Element**

Water

**Corresponding Planet**

Venus

**Zodiac Sign**

Cancer

**Upright Meaning**

Love, mutual attraction, happiness, partnerships, relationships, unified love, connection, mutual respect, peace, marriage, engagements, proposals, soulmates, fairness, alignment, compatibility, and passion.

**Reversed Meaning**

Disharmony, arguments, distrust, anguish, self-love, strained relationships, breakups, separations, divorces, bullying, discord, dominance, abuse, ending friendships, inequity, fights, and unhappy marriages.

## Three of Cups

**Element**

Water

**Corresponding Planet**

Mercury

**Zodiac Sign**

Cancer

**Upward Meaning**

Friendships, happiness, joy, celebration, creativity, good conversation, collaboration, happy times, meetings, graduation, social gatherings, engagement parties, weddings, enjoyments, indulgences, and festivals.

**Reversed Meaning**

Cheating, independence, frustration, alone time, gossiping, extreme partying, lack of excitement, overindulgence, isolation, loneliness, lack of social life, freedom, affairs, and termination.

# Four of Cups

**Element**

Water

**Corresponding Planet**

Moon

**Zodiac Sign**

Cancer

**Upward Meaning**

Depression, meditation, feeling stuck, apathy, missed opportunities, re-evaluation, turning down offers, regrets, contemplation, self-absorption, negativity, boredom, disillusion, nostalgia, apathy, remorse, stagnation, frustration, and missed opportunities.

**Reversed Meaning**

Passion, withdrawal, taking action, enthusiasm, moving forward, retreat, being proactive, getting over regrets, interest, gratitude, focus, motivation, self-awareness, end of stagnation, optimism, and seizing the moment.

# Five of Cups

**Element**

Water

**Corresponding Planet**

Pluto

**Zodiac Sign**

Scorpio

**Upward Meaning**

Pessimism, loss, regret, failure, sadness, disappointment, grief, trauma, remorse, sorrow, guilt, tragedy, rejection, unwanted change, despair, missed opportunities, emotional immaturity, misery, and negativity.

**Reversed Meaning**

Acceptance, moving on, forgiveness, overcoming sorrow, peace, healing, setbacks, releasing emotions, accepting help, getting over hopelessness, moving forward, trauma recovery, and being sociable.

## Six of Cups

**Element**

Water

**Corresponding Planet**

The Sun

**Zodiac Sign**

Scorpio

**Upward Meaning**

Innocence, carefree, playful, nostalgic, innocence, joyful, childhood memories, reunions, children, memories, freshness, melancholy, purity, longing, creativity, the impact of the past, protection, compassion, support, goodwill, family, simplicity, gifts, sharing, childhood, and immaturity.

**Reversed Meaning**

Forgiveness, independence, maturity, boredom, leaving home, living in the past, immobility, lack of playfulness, childhood issues, growing up, monotony, and a lack of imagination.

## Seven of Cups

**Element**

Water

**Corresponding Planet**

Pluto

**Zodiac Sign**

Scorpio

**Upward Meaning**

Multiple options, meditation, illusions, fantasy, opportunities, choices, wishful thinking, decisions, hallucinations, possibilities, procrastination, imagination, and dreaming.

**Reversed Meaning**

Acceptance, reality, alignment, forgiveness, finding peace, overwhelming options, bad choices, clarity, healing, personal values, shallowness, reality, lost opportunities, sobriety, decisiveness, being trapped, and a lack of spiritual growth.

# Eight of Cups

**Element**

Water

**Corresponding Planet**

Neptune

**Zodiac Sign**

Pisces

**Upward Meaning**

Fatigue, escapism, traveling, introspection, abandonment, letting go, disappointment, disconnecting, withdrawal, cowardice, self-analysis, letting go, and reaching your limit.

**Reversed Meaning**

Stagnation, unreal happiness, fear of the unknown, inability to move on, trying, drifting aimlessly, indecision, clinginess, living in toxicity, monotony, staying, self-doubt, and lack of self-awareness.

# Nine of Cups

**Element**

Water

**Corresponding Planet**

Neptune

**Zodiac Sign**

Pisces

**Upward Meaning**

Joy, happiness, rewards, making dreams come true, accomplishments, fulfilling wishes, prosperity, positivity, gratitude, satisfaction, contentment, abundance, cheer, success, and optimism.

### Reversed Meaning

Pain, pessimism, nightmares, grief, broken dreams, failure, destruction, indulgence, disadvantage, lack of accomplishment, materialism, dissatisfaction, misery, low self-confidence, negativity, disappointment, and unsatisfied feelings.

## Ten of Cups

### Element
Water

### Corresponding Planet
Neptune

### Zodiac Sign
Pisces

### Upright Meaning
Harmony, joy, marriage, imagination, happiness, children, partnerships, family, karma, prosperity, reunions, domestic bliss, alignment, divine love, security, fulfilling relationships, stability, abundance, playfulness, compassion, happy endings, best friends, and good fortune.

### Reversed Meaning
Conflict, disagreements, infertility, despair, separation, divorce, incompatibility, broken family, dissociation, difficult relationships, broken values, unconventional families, instability, and toxic families.

## Page of Cups

### Element
Water

### Corresponding Planet
Moon

### Zodiac Sign
Cancer

### Upright Meaning
Possibilities, loyalty, dreams, idealism, kindness, naivety, curiosity, inner voice, happy news, feeling young, emotional maturity, kids, creativity, intuition, opportunities, sensitivity, inner child, loyalty, and engagements.

**Reversed Meaning**

Immaturity, attention seeking, vulnerability, ideas, unfulfilled dreams, childhood issues, sexuality, jealousy, obsession, bad news, childishness, creativity block, ignoring your gut, and seduction.

# Knight of Cups

**Element**

Water

**Corresponding Planet**

Neptune

**Zodiac Sign**

Pisces

**Upright Meaning**

Beauty, grace, offers, romance, chivalry, invitations, negotiation, charm, gentleness, listening to your heart, tact, imagination, creativity, idealism, action, and peacefulness.

**Reversed Meaning**

Heartbreak, obsession, envy, cheating, deception, jealousy, disappointment, mood swings, overactive imagination, turmoil, unrealistic, undiplomatic, superficiality, irritability, and procrastination.

# Queen of Cups

**Element**

Water

**Corresponding Planet**

Neptune

**Zodiac Sign**

Cancer

**Upright Meaning**

Warmth, maturity, caring, shyness, female instinct, kindness, comfort, sensitivity, empathy, femininity, loyalty, love, womanhood, compassion, stability, intuition, safety, healing, joy, beauty, courage, respect, giving advice, nurturing.

### Reversed Meaning

Superficiality, lack of trust, neediness, weakness, insecurity, untrustworthy, melancholy, co-dependent, self-love, immaturity, over-sensitivity, and smothering.

## King of Cups

### Element
Water

### Corresponding Planet
Neptune

### Zodiac Sign
Pisces

### Upright Meaning
Creativity, loyalty, compassion, faithfulness, wisdom, sympathy, tolerance, consideration, dependability, harmony, diplomacy, emotional balance, passion, and simplicity.

### Reverse Meaning
Bad advice, controlling, intolerance, unfriendly, emotional, unreliable, stress, unproductive, naivety, nervousness, manipulation, indifference, mood swings, depression, withdrawal, and instability.

## Suit of Swords

### Keywords
Communication, intellect, ideas, logic.

### Element
Air

### Alternative Names
Spades

### Jungian Function
Thinking

The Suit of Swords tarot focuses on your intellect, mind, and thoughts. They represent logical thinking, communication skills, and applying reason to any situation. When these cards are strong in your reading, they influence your communication skills and self-expression. However, when they are weak, they make you confused, cold, and aggressive.

# Ace of Swords

**Element**
Air

**Corresponding Planet**
Venus

**Zodiac Sign**
Libra

**Upright Meaning**
Clarity, triumph, focus, breakthrough, force, opportunities, intensity, success, intellect, concentration, excitement, new ideas, beginnings, and communication.

**Reverse Meaning**
Lack of productivity, misunderstandings, injustice, frustration, destruction, creativity block, insults, lost opportunities, inability to focus, poor communication skills, forgetfulness, and failures.

# Two of Swords

**Element**
Air

**Corresponding Planet**
Venus

**Zodiac Sign**
Libra

**Upright Meaning**
Avoidance, resistance, struggling with making decisions, feeling concerned, and reconciliation.

**Reverse Meaning**
Indecision, anger, disruptions, deception, cancellations, emotional detachment, anxiety, work overload, confusion, tension, and caution.

# Three of Swords

**Element**

Air

**Corresponding Planet**

Venus

**Zodiac Sign**

Libra

**Upright Meaning**

Loss, separation, treason, heartbreak, withdrawal, sadness, absence, pain, division, loss, isolation, depression, misery, sadness, grief, confusion, and distraction.

**Reverse Meaning**

Negative inner voice, moving on, forgiveness, optimism, letting go of pain, suppressing feelings, overcoming adversity, and compromising.

# Four of Swords

**Element**

Air

**Corresponding Planet**

Venus

**Zodiac Sign**

Libra

**Upright Meaning**

Planning for the future, relaxation, introspection, making good decisions, retreat, worry, meditation, opportunities, stress, clarity, anxiety, breakthrough, rest, contemplation, need for solitude, recovery, peacefulness, and frustration.

**Reverse Meaning**

Renewal, rising, exhaustion, irrationality, peace, restlessness, destruction, lack of productivity, healing, stagnation, loss of faith, and coming out of isolation.

# Five of Swords

**Element**

Air

**Corresponding Planet**

Pluto

**Zodiac Sign**

Scorpio

**Upright Meaning**

Arguments, failure, battle, transformation, defeat, conflict, competition, deception, aggression, winning, lying, and bullying.

**Reverse Meaning**

Compromising, communicating, getting in trouble, solutions, paying for mistakes, sacrifices, violence, moving on, vengeance, reconciliation, fixing mistakes, risky behavior, and reducing stress.

# Six of Swords

**Element**

Air

**Corresponding Planet**

Mercury

**Zodiac Sign**

Aquarius

**Upright Meaning**

Making peace, transition, healing, travel, escapism, moving on, change, improvement, stability, trips, and overcoming hardships.

**Reverse Meaning**

Feeling trapped, recovering, overwhelmed, unable to change, and lacking progress.

# Seven of Swords

**Element**

Air

**Corresponding Planet**

Uranus

**Zodiac Sign**

Aquarius

**Upright Meaning**

Lying, strategy, betrayal, manipulation, deceit, stealing, cheating, spying, escaping responsibility, trickery, adaptability, and taking risks.

**Reverse Meaning**

Being accountable, confessing, starting over, deceiving yourself, being a secret keeper, turning over a new leaf, making plans, and taking action.

# Eight of Swords

**Element**

Air

**Corresponding Planet**

Jupiter

**Zodiac Sign**

Gemini

**Upright Meaning**

Unproductive, fear, imprisonment, negativity, drama, feeling stuck, difficulty, restrictions, feeling powerless, emergency, hopelessness, victim mentality, losing your voice, weakness, and anxiety.

**Reverse Meaning**

Escapism, hope, being in control, new perspectives, freedom, negative inner voice, surviving trauma, honesty, empowerment, productivity, letting go of negativity, healing, letting go of anxiety, confronting your fears, and believing in yourself.

# Nine of Swords

**Element**
Air

**Corresponding Planet**
Mars

**Zodiac Sign**
Gemini

**Upright Meaning**
Despair, nightmares, regret, panic, anxiety, worry, remorse, negativity, overreaction, dissatisfaction, feeling overwhelmed, hopelessness, fears, burden, and guilt.

**Reverse Meaning**
Clarity, improvement, secrets, optimism, recovery, overcoming fears, turmoil, coping mechanisms, helping others, and conflict.

# Ten of Swords

**Element**
Air

**Corresponding Planet**
Mars

**Zodiac Sign**
Gemini

**Upright Meaning**
Financial problems, laziness, backstabbing, resentment, sad endings, failing, wounds, enemies, betrayal, complaining, loss, breakdowns, crises, disasters, and hitting rock bottom.

**Reverse Meaning**
Perseverance, overcoming trauma, rebirth, starting something new, new coping mechanisms, improvement, and learning from your mistakes.

# Page of Swords

**Element**

Air

**Corresponding Planet**

Mercury

**Zodiac Sign**

Gemini

**Upright Meaning**

Inspiration, planning, high self-esteem, caution, justice, youthfulness, protection, communication skills, curiosity, ideas, knowledge, and thinking.

**Reverse Meaning**

Lack of productivity, living in a fantasy world, manipulation, paranoia, silliness, defensiveness, burnout, mind games, expressing oneself, being in a rush, and not taking action.

# Knight of Swords

**Element**

Air

**Corresponding Planet**

Mercury

**Zodiac Sign**

Libra

**Upright Meaning**

Changes, focus, courage, bravery, accomplishment, rebellion, persistence, adventure, honesty, impulsiveness, intelligence, wit, ambition, success, taking action, impatient, and seizing opportunities.

**Reverse Meaning**

Self-doubt, aggression, restfulness, stagnation, cruelty, laziness, lost opportunities, lack of focus, exhaustion, loss of control, poor manners, assertiveness, and danger.

# Queen of Swords

**Element**

Air

**Corresponding Planet**

Uranus

**Zodiac Sign**

Libra

**Upright Meaning**

Support, honesty, empathy, justice, protection, strength, talkative, funny, morals, independence, boundaries, communication skills, unbiased judgment, wit, solving problems, and sadness.

**Reverse Meaning**

Carelessness, pessimism, cruelty, gossip, danger, manipulation, cold heart, resentment, emotions, vengefulness, dishonesty, and cheating.

# King of Swords

**Element**

Air

**Corresponding Planet**

Saturn

**Zodiac Sign**

Aquarius

**Upright Meaning**

Fatherhood, honesty, structure, authority, routine, leadership, intelligence, logic, clarity, truth, conversation, power, strength, integrity, and morals.

**Reverse Meaning**

Behaving irrationally, tyranny, abuse of power, brutality, immorality, aggression, manipulation, violence, power, lack of discipline, and cynicism.

# The Suit of Pentacles

**Keywords**

Stability, materialism, nature, and physical body.

**Element**

Earth

**Alternative Names**

Discs and coins

**Jungian Function**

Sensation

The suit of pentacles cards focuses on one's perception of the world around them and how one shapes their reality. The cards represent your ego and self-esteem. When these cards are strong, they represent your strength and optimism during adversity. When they are weak, they reflect laziness and stubbornness.

# Ace of Pentacles

**Element**

Earth

**Corresponding Planet**

Saturn

**Zodiac Sign**

Capricorn

**Upright Meaning**

Gaining money, abundance, investments, prosperity, manifestation, stability, beginnings, new opportunities, new career, and comfort.

**Reverse Meaning**

Negativity, greed, frustration, instability, missed opportunities, insecurity, and inability to plan.

# Two of Pentacles

**Element**

Earth

**Corresponding Planet**

Saturn

**Zodiac Sign**

Capricorn

**Upright Meaning**

Balance, flexibility, adaptability, perseverance, resourcefulness, multi-tasking, and time management.

**Reverse Meaning**

Imbalance, chaos, bad organization skills, messiness, over-commitment, and feeling overwhelmed.

## Three of Pentacles

**Element**

Earth

**Corresponding Planet**

Saturn

**Zodiac Sign**

Capricorn

**Upright Meaning**

Growth, common goals, teamwork, learning, recognition, collaboration, and effort.

**Reverse Meaning**

Lack of motivation, ego, disharmony, conflict, lack of ambition, apathy, working solo, and competition.

## Four of Pentacles

**Element**

Earth

**Corresponding Planet**

Saturn

**Zodiac Sign**

Capricorn

**Upright Meaning**

Desire for control, possessiveness, security, materialism, saving, inability to change, boundaries, stability, acting conservatively, control, and wealth.

**Reverse Meaning**

Generosity, greed, acceptance, letting go of the past, relinquishing control, openness, overspending, and giving.

## Five of Pentacles

**Element**

Earth

**Corresponding Planet**

Venus

**Zodiac Sign**

Taurus

**Upright Meaning**

Financial troubles, loss, anxiety, lack of faith, abandonment, solitude, illness, poverty, adversity, rejection, struggling, hardships, disgrace, and unemployment.

**Reverse Meaning**

Victory, luck, health, financial gain, recovery, positive changes, forgiveness, and overcoming adversity.

## Six of Pentacles

**Element**

Earth

**Corresponding Planet**

Venus

**Zodiac Sign**

Taurus

**Upright Meaning**

Generosity, support, charity, balance, giving, prosperity, gratitude, receiving, and community.

**Reverse Meaning**

Debt, desperation, self-care, extortion, and inequality.

## Seven of Pentacles

**Element**
Earth

**Corresponding Planet**
Venus

**Zodiac Sign**
Taurus

**Upright Meaning**
Hard work, patience, investment, harvest, success, results, perseverance, rewards, progress, planning, and growth.

**Reverse Meaning**
Impatience, waste, delay, laziness, setbacks, poor planning, procrastination, and lack of growth.

## Eight of Pentacles

**Element**
Earth

**Corresponding Planet**
Mercury

**Zodiac Sign**
Virgo

**Upright Meaning**
Ambition, quality, perfection, expertise, talent, commitment, developing skills, accomplishment, dedication, repeating tasks, and high standards.

**Reverse Meaning**
Bad reputation, workaholic, development, laziness, and lack of motivation.

## Nine of Pentacles

**Element**
Earth

**Corresponding Planet**
Mercury

**Zodiac Sign**

Virgo

**Upright Meaning**

Independence, rewards, abundance, success, comfort, achievement, luxury, leisure, prosperity, and financial security.

**Reverse Meaning**

Feeling stuck, shallowness, success, pride, reckless spending, self-worth, over-investment, and financial instability.

## Ten of Pentacles

**Element**

Earth

**Corresponding Planet**

Mercury

**Zodiac Sign**

Virgo

**Upright Meaning**

Inheritance, wealth, tradition, legacy, success, ancestry, family, foundations, contribution, financial security, privilege, and stability.

**Reverse Meaning**

Financial troubles, bankruptcy, family issues, instability, separation, limitation, loss, debt, and breaking traditions.

## Page of Pentacles

**Element**

Earth

**Corresponding Planet**

Venus

**Zodiac Sign**

Taurus

**Upright Meaning**

Faithfulness, ambition, manifestation, planning, accomplishing your goals, practicality, consistency, and developing skills.

**Reverse Meaning**

Procrastination, irresponsibility, immaturity, unattainable goals, lack of progress, foolishness, and underachieving.

# Knight of Pentacles

**Element**

Earth

**Corresponding Planet**

Mercury

**Zodiac Sign**

Virgo

**Upright Meaning**

Improvement, routine, consistency, efficiency, hard work, strong will, patience, productivity, and commitment.

**Reverse Meaning**

Laziness, irresponsibility, perfection, stubbornness, boredom, trapped, dullness, gambling, and possessiveness.

# Queen of Pentacles

**Element**

Earth

**Corresponding Planet**

Saturn

**Zodiac Sign**

Capricorn

**Upright Meaning**

Down to earth, generosity, comfort, caretaker, healing, nurturing, security, sensible, success, and prosperity.

**Reverse Meaning**

Self-care, smothering, dependence, envy, intolerant, selfishness, jealousy, greed, and insecurity.

## King of Pentacles

**Element**

Earth

**Corresponding Planet**

Saturn

**Zodiac Sign**

Capricorn

**Upright Meaning**

Security, reliability, wealth, sensuality, feeling grounded, provider, business, protection, stability, abundance, and discipline.

**Reverse Meaning**

Instability, gambling, corruption, possessiveness, materialism, greed, stubbornness, and bad financial decisions.

## Suit of Wands

**Keywords**

Power, willpower, drive, creativity, and energy.

**Element**

Fire

**Alternative Names**

Scepters, clubs, or rods

**Jungian Function**

Intuition

The suit of wand cards represents your day-to-day activities. When they are strong, they fill you with passion and courage and drive you to take action. However, when the cards are weak, you become reckless, dangerous, and destructive.

## Ace of Wands

**Element**

Fire

**Corresponding Planet**

Mars

**Zodiac Sign**

Aries

**Upright Meaning**

Breakthrough, growth, challenge, new beginnings, potential, great ideas, inspiration, fertility, creativity, action, good news, enthusiasm, travel, and boldness.

**Reverse Meaning**

Abuse of power, disappointment, delays, predictability, hesitation, irrationality, distractions, boredom, infertility, lack of morals, lack of direction, and lost opportunity.

## Two of Wands

**Element**

Fire

**Corresponding Planet**

Mars

**Zodiac Sign**

Aries

**Upright Meaning**

Decisions, anticipation, discovery, waiting, power, restlessness, progress, withdrawal, partnership, detachment, choices, and planning for the future.

**Reverse Meaning**

Sudden change, indecisiveness, fear of the unknown, uncertainty, goals, poor planning, and limitation.

## Three of Wands

**Element**

Fire

**Corresponding Planet**

Sun

**Zodiac Sign**

Aries

### Upright Meaning

Exploration, success, progress, leadership skills, freedom, foresight, moving on, traveling, self-esteem, planning for the future, growth, and living life to the fullest.

### Reverse Meaning

Regret, self-doubt, poor planning, lack of foresight, inability to grow, restrictions, bad choices, being haunted by the past, and low self-esteem.

## Four of Wands

### Element
Fire

### Corresponding Planet
Venus

### Zodiac Sign
Aries

### Upright Meaning

Celebration, joy, reunion, homecoming, gathering, excitement, stability, teamwork, security, weddings, success, harmony, events, relaxation, belonging, pride, and surprises.

### Reverse Meaning

Walking away, insecurity, transition, cancellations, sad family life, conflict, loneliness, and instability.

## Five of Wands

### Element
Fire

### Corresponding Planet
Saturn

### Zodiac Sign
Leo

### Upright Meaning

Challenges, struggle, conflict, fighting, disagreements, battle, tension, rivalry, diversity, arguments, aggression, opposition, petty, chaos.

**Reverse Meaning**

Compromise, peace, avoiding conflict, harmony, truce, teamwork, solutions, releasing tension, focus, and shyness.

## Six of Wands

**Element**

Fire

**Corresponding Planet**

Jupiter

**Zodiac Sign**

Leo

**Upright Meaning**

Victory, pride, progress, triumph, rewards, winning, fame, self-esteem, praise, recognition, acclaim, success, accomplishments, support, and goodwill,

**Reverse Meaning**

Failure, disgrace, weakness, broken promises, betrayal, ego, lack of support, arrogance, low self-esteem, disappointment, bad intentions, and lack of achievement.

## Seven of Wands

**Element**

Fire

**Corresponding Planet**

Mars

**Zodiac Sign**

Leo

**Upright Meaning**

Conviction, challenge, determination, competition, defiance, protection, strong will, assertiveness, self-defense, stamina, and dominance.

**Reverse Meaning**

Burnout, compromise, solutions, teamwork, feeling overwhelmed, weakness, surrender, defeat, and lack of respect.

# Eight of Wands

**Element**

Fire

**Corresponding Planet**

Mercury

**Zodiac Sign**

Sagittarius

**Upright Meaning**

Excitement, speed, taking action, making fast decisions, travel, thrill, excitement, movement, quick changes, progress, freedom, and solutions.

**Reverse Meaning**

Limitations, impatience, frustration, negativity, delays, slow progress, inability to change, and lost opportunities.

# Nine of Wands

**Element**

Fire

**Corresponding Planet**

Moon

**Zodiac Sign**

Sagittarius

**Upright Meaning**

Perseverance, grit, protection, exhaustion, bravery, battle, resilience, boundaries, persistence, resilience, and being easily hurt.

**Reverse Meaning**

Inability to compromise, retreat, struggle, withdraw, feel overwhelmed, give up, paranoia, defensiveness, and stubbornness.

# Ten of Wands

**Element**

Fire

**Corresponding Planet**

Saturn

**Zodiac Sign**

Sagittarius

**Upright Meaning**

Struggle, obligation, hard work, duty, responsibility, restriction, burden, delays, completion, and resistance.

**Reverse Meaning**

Stress, breakdowns, problems, release, delegation, and challenges.

# Page of Wands

**Element**

Fire

**Corresponding Planet**

Jupiter

**Zodiac Sign**

Sagittarius

**Upright Meaning**

Cheerfulness, positive thoughts, free spirit, confidence, ideas, good news, inspiration, fearlessness, extroversion, discovery, energy, excitement, creativity, potential, adventure, optimism, intelligence, and playfulness.

**Reverse Meaning**

Ill intentions, naivety, impatience, new ideas, spiritual path, haste, laziness, low energy, outbursts, low self-esteem, boredom, and fearfulness.

# Knight of Wands

**Element**

Fire

**Corresponding Planet**

Jupiter

**Zodiac Sign**

Sagittarius

**Upright Meaning**

Charm, bravery, passion, heroism, confidence, hot temper, independence, rebellion, free spirit, impulsiveness, warmth, adventure, confidence, energy, and open-mindedness.

**Reverse Meaning**

Arrogance, controlling, shallowness, passive, restlessness, impatience, frustrations, abuse, competition, delays, aggression, haste, violence, recklessness, enthusiasm.

## Queen of Wands

**Element**

Fire

**Corresponding Planet**

Mars

**Zodiac Sign**

Aries

**Upright Meaning**

Attraction, energy, bravery, humor, passion, cheerfulness, confidence, friendliness, wholeheartedness, charisma, optimism, independence, social, strength, determination, and motherhood.

**Reverse Meaning**

Volatility, infertility, self-respect, deception, jealousy, unfaithfulness, introversion, spite, selfishness, manipulation, insecurity, vengeance, and self-righteousness.

## King of Wands

**Element**

Fire

**Corresponding Planet**

Mars

**Zodiac Sign**

Leo

**Upright Meaning**

Protection, optimism, honor, experience, innovation, excitement, vision, confidence, inspiration, charm, entrepreneur, friendliness, energy, fear, responsibility, leadership skills, taking action, magnetism, control, and loyalty.

**Reverse Meaning**

Selfishness, control, force, manipulation, extremism, poor manners, bullying, impulsiveness, abuse, broken promises, expectations, ruthlessness, domination, and flirting.

The Minor Arcana tarot cards are significant in your reading as they can open your eyes to issues that impact your daily life. Pay attention to them when you get them in your reading, as there is always a useful message to be had.

# Chapter 4: Connecting with the Cards

Through their powerful images and symbols, tarot cards help us gain insight and understanding into our lives. However, many people find it difficult or don't understand how necessary it is to connect with their spread and use their full potential. Connecting with the cards leads to deeper insights and more accurate readings. With practice, you can learn how to trust your intuition and better understand the messages they reveal. This chapter will provide tips on establishing a deeper affinity with your tarot cards. You will learn how to cleanse the cards to reinstate energy and how to attune your spread for divination and readings.

It is important to connect with your cards to have a successful reading.[36]

### What Does a Strong Connection Feel Like?

A strong connection with your tarot cards can be likened to a relationship with a partner, friends, or family. When you first start speaking with a new friend, you might need help expressing yourself. As you continue the conversation, you become more comfortable, and your words flow more naturally. Similarly, connecting with your tarot cards will make you more confident and fluent in their language, energy, and messages. You will also feel more confident interpreting your cards to maximize their wisdom and guidance. And sure enough, a strong connection will feel exactly like the one you have with someone you respect and admire.

## How to Connect Your Intuition to the Deck

In order to fully connect with your tarot cards, you must bridge your conscious and unconscious mind. One of the best ways to do this is to spend time with them. Bring the images and symbols of the spread to life by holding them in your hands, running your fingers along their edges, and feeling their weight. Actively visualize yourself in the scenes you see to weave your own interpretation into your readings. For example, suppose you get the Five of Wands (conflict and change), and it brings up feelings of frustration. In that case, you can weave an experience from your life into your reading to connect to the card. Perhaps you have felt frustrated with an assignment at work or school. By weaving your memories and emotions into each card, you connect them with your own life experiences, activating their power.

### Spend Quality Time with Them

By sleeping with the cards close to you, you will be able to focus more deeply on the meanings behind their messages. This will also help you open yourself up to the power and possibilities the cards reveal. You can leave them next to you (wherever you leave your phone) or keep them under your pillow. Before going to sleep, take a few moments to meditate and focus on the cards. If one comes to mind, go with the thought, and try to imagine the specifics of the card. Specifics include color, shapes, and message. This will allow you to be open to the messages that they give you. Then when you wake up in the morning, take a few moments to reflect on any messages you received while sleeping. And consider why these messages relate to the cards.

## Examine Each Card

Examining the cards in a tarot deck can be both a thrilling and daunting experience. To ensure that you become attuned to your spread, take time to examine each card thoroughly. Be aware of any feelings, thoughts, or images that come to your mind.

1. Start by looking at the artwork on the card.
2. Note any symbols, colors, people, and animals that appear in the image.
3. Then, read the card's description and associated keywords.
4. Spend some time meditating on the card, allowing yourself to draw connections between the artwork and the meaning.
5. To deepen your understanding of the card, journal your thoughts and feelings on the card.

These days, most spreads come with an accompanying booklet describing the nuances of each card. And although they can be useful for beginners to understand what the cards are supposed to mean, once you connect with them, they might start saying more to you. If this happens, this is a good sign. It means the spread is speaking to you.

As you examine each card, ask yourself the following question to establish a connection and alignment with them:

- Are there any recurring symbols or motifs? If so, how does this recurrence make you feel? And why do you think that is?
- Do they have different names from other decks you've seen? If so, does this bring a new meaning to them? Make them unique to you?
- Is there a color theme? If so, do these colors resonate with you, and why?
- Are there any cards you like or dislike more than others? If so, why?

Remember that there is no right or wrong answer to these questions. The aim is for you to establish feelings about the spread themselves. This will help you to connect with them more. Like when we meet someone we like, we can't stop thinking about them, and it makes us feel closer to them.

### Shuffle the Spread

Flip through a new tarot spread, and you'll feel a sense of anticipation and excitement. As you shuffle them, pay attention to how they look and feel in your hands. It's best to do this while sitting down. If you haven't shuffled before or aren't very good at it, as the cards fall, they will fall close to you, not to the floor. Don't feel pressured to get this right on your first attempt. As you practice and get to know the cards, shuffling them will become easier for you.

- A deck of tarot cards can be quite substantial, with a luxurious feel
- They have a texture that is both soft and inviting yet firm and sturdy
- Their artwork can be beautiful and carefully designed to convey the various meanings in the spread
- When you flip through the cards, notice symbols, archetypes, and images that you are familiar with
- Each card has its own unique meaning and can often evoke intense feelings and subtle energies
- As you hold the cards in your hands, take note of the power of the symbols and artwork.

You might also be drawn to some of the cards depending on the tarot spread. As you go through them, you might find that some cards have more meaning for you than others, and this can be a clue for how you can use the deck to harness their powers.

A sense of energy or calm might also come from the spread as a whole, which can be very calming and meditative as you explore its depths.

### The Interview Spread

The Interview Spread is a popular technique used by tarot readers to gain insight into their tarot spread. Because every card in the spread has a unique meaning and interpretation, spend time familiarizing yourself with the individual personalities of each one. Not just visually, as you have done so far, but emotionally. Interviewing the spread is a fun yet insightful way to do this. Treat this as though you were talking to a new friend. What can you ask that will make you know your friends (spreads) intentions towards you?

You can lay the cards out however you want. Lay them out in a spread of six (like a diamond shape) or keep them in a pile and pick one at a time. Go through each card and ask the following questions. It will also be useful for you to write down what answers you get. This will help to formalize your thoughts, as well as track your learning process. You'll find you get more answers the more you do this method.

1. What is your defining characteristic?
2. What are your strengths?
3. What are your limitations?
4. What work can we do together?
5. What can you teach me?

### Care for Them

Taking the time to properly care for your cards helps to show your appreciation for the power of tarot and the insights they can provide. They are powerful tools of divination and so should be treated with reverence. To show your respect and appreciation, take the time to properly store and care for your spread. Storing your cards with respect is essential to keep them in the best condition and ensure they are as effective as possible when using them. The best way to store them is to keep them in a special box or pouch designed for this purpose. It should be lined with cloth or velvet and have a lid to keep out dust and debris. The cards should be placed in the box in a meaningful way; some practitioners like to arrange them by suit, others by color. If you use a pouch, you should ensure it is large enough for all the cards and closed securely to keep them from slipping out.

### Use Them

As you become familiar with each card's personality, don't forget to use the deck as a whole. While each offers something different, the deck as a whole provides guidance, advice, and spiritual insight that can be used as a tool for self-discovery and personal growth. Try giving yourself a personal reading. Choose a spread that you feel comfortable with, then draw the cards relevant to the situation you would like guidance on. You can then interpret the cards and their meanings to gain insight.

# How to Cleanse Your Cards

Cleansing your tarot cards is essential to maintaining their energy and keeping them in good condition. They hold many of our secrets, insights, and intuitions, and keeping them strong and clean is vital. Tarot card cleansing can be a simple yet meaningful ritual that helps you connect with your cards and create a sacred space for them. There are various methods for cleansing tarot cards, from using crystals to visualization and affirmations. Each method can have powerful psychic results; choose the one that resonates with you the most.

### What Does It Mean to Cleanse?

The act of cleansing involves ritually clearing space and removing energy from your cards so you can use them with a clean slate. With each new reading, you are adding your imprint on the cards. They become infused with both your energy and the energy of the people for whom you are doing the reading. But cleansing can help you remove any unwanted energy, so you can create a clean space for your cards and a fresh start for each new reading. Cleansing your cards can be done at any point and isn't just necessary before a reading. You can also use cleansing to connect to your cards and create a sacred space for them. This can be a meaningful, spiritual experience that will help you to develop an even stronger bond with your cards.

### Why Is Cleansing Necessary?

As you invoke the act of divination for readings, you are adding your imprint on your cards, but this can also make them less pure and less connected to your intuition. Over time, your cards can become weighed down by your energy, impatience, and other emotions, which can make them less effective for future readings. Cleansing your cards helps you to clear any negative energy that might be weighing them down so you can create a fresh space for divine reading. It also helps you connect to your intuition and strengthens your bond with your cards. This can help you to trust your readings more and use them in a much more intuitive and confident way.

# Cleansing Methods

There are many ways to cleanse your cards that will fit your way of life. Some methods are more focused than others, so take time to choose the one that's right for you and where you are in your journey. With the right method, you can create a powerful divination experience that will leave a lasting impact on your cards and your readings.

### Sage Smoke

One of the most common cleansing methods is to use the smoke from burning sage to remove energy from your cards. You can use a smudge stick, incense, or a sage bowl to burn the sage and then use the smoke to gently wave the cards around. As the smoke wafts around your cards, it will cleanse any negative energy and leave your cards refreshed and ready for a new reading.

### Visualization and Affirmations

This method is a great choice if you are new to cleansing and would like to try something simple and effective.

1. Hold your deck in your hands, close your eyes, and visualize a sweeping gesture that erases the cards' energies.
2. Another way to do this visually is to imagine yourself pulling the energy away from the deck of cards and throwing it up in the air.
3. For affirmations, there is no hard and fast rule for this. Remember that these cards are now a part of you, so you need to tell them something reassuring as well as firm for them to know that they need to start afresh.

### Crystals

Using crystals to cleanse your tarot cards can be a great way to combine cleansing and other rituals you might already be doing. You can use crystals to cleanse your cards when you are doing a reading or at any other time when you want to clean them. Hold the crystals in your hands, and then gently pass the cards through the energy of the crystals. You can also place the crystals on top of or beside the cards for an added boost of energy. Cleansing crystals include:

- Amethyst
- Rose Quartz
- Selenite
- Black Obsidian

When selecting a cleansing method, don't forget to choose one that resonates with you and to which you feel connected. Cleansing can be a very meaningful and spiritual experience, so choosing a method that helps you reach that higher level of connection and spirituality is essential.

## How to Attune Your Cards for Divination

Attuning your deck is an essential step in the divination process and can help you to get the most out of your readings. Attuning is a simple process that requires you to create a connection between yourself and your tarot deck. You can think of it as a way of "tuning in" to the vibrations of your deck and "adjusting" your energy to align with the energy of the cards. It can be done with an intention, a ritual, or a blessing, depending on what feels right for you. When you attune your deck, you create a safe and sacred space for your readings and allow yourself to be more open to the messages the cards offer. Attuning also creates a deeper understanding of the cards, allowing you to further explore their meanings. So, if you want to get the most out of your tarot readings, attuning your deck is a must!

### Preparation for Attunement

The first step in attuning your tarot deck is to prepare yourself. You can do this in your room, at your altar, or somewhere else that feels right for you.

1. First, you will want to be away from any noise and distractions. Ensure you are in a quiet environment where you will be free from interruptions.
2. Next, make sure that you have enough space for you to feel comfortable and relaxed.
3. You can also create a sacred space by burning incense, lighting candles, or meditating.
4. Then prepare yourself before you begin the attunement process by deciding on an intention for your deck.

An *intention* is something that you would like to bring out of your deck and into your life. It can be something you wish to improve on, something that you would like more of in your life, or the wishes of someone you are reading for. This can be anything from a wish for financial prosperity to the desire to feel more confident in social situations, so the possibilities are endless! You can also choose to create a ritual or use a blessing for your deck if that feels more appropriate for you.

### Energy Method

When you are ready to begin, hold the card in your hand and sense the energy coming from it. What do you feel? How does it feel against your hand? What sounds, smells, or sights can you pick up from the card? Once you have identified the energy that is coming from the card, use your intention to attune the rest of your deck.

### Focus Method

This method is a bit more involved but can be very helpful if you are having difficulty connecting with your deck. When you are ready, focus on the card and try to feel what is coming from it. Visualize the card and try to see it in your mind's eye. This can be difficult at first, but it will get easier with practice. Once you have seen the card, try to focus on the feelings that you are receiving from it. Again, what do you feel? What emotions are coming from the card? What sensations are you picking up from it? Then, use your intention to attune your deck.

Connecting with your tarot cards is essential to understanding and interpreting their meanings. While the cards themselves are only a small part of the overall journey of self-discovery, they can provide powerful insight into our lives and can assist us in gaining clarity and understanding. With regular use and practice, you, too, will develop an intuitive understanding of the cards and how they relate to your life. By connecting with the cards and asking questions, you'll understand how different forces impact you and gain clarity on difficult decisions. Now, connect to access the wisdom of your higher self and unlock access to insights to positively shape your life.

# Chapter 5: How to Read the Cards

Every Tarot reading is a journey, like reading a book or peeking into a reality you have not lived. Tarot readings give you insight, inform you of blessings, and give you warnings at times.

It is common for beginners to feel overwhelmed at first. This is a normal reaction, given the amount of knowledge that they have to learn before they can read for themselves as others. However, the beautiful thing about tarot reading is that one gets better with practice and time.

There are several factors to take into consideration before you start a reading.[27]

In this chapter, you will find everything you need to read Tarot cards. Not only will you know how to prepare yourself for a reading, but you will also learn how to interpret the cards and what different cards combination mean together.

# Intuition

One of the vital tools that you will use while reading the cards is your intuition. Studying Tarot is one thing, and integrating your intuition with reading cards is another. For instance, you can have each card memorized, but this does not make you a tarot reader. A tarot reader integrates their intuition with the reading.

Intuition is often referred to as "gut feeling." It is a voice that emits from your being, and the more you attune yourself to it, the louder and clearer you can hear it. Every human has intuition, but not everyone makes use of it.

### How Can You Enhance Your Intuition?

Frequent meditation can help you sharpen your intuition. The more you meditate and pay attention to your body and emotions, the more you can listen to your intuition. Find a quiet place in your house and sit in a comfortable position. Close your eyes and relax your muscles and bones. Regulate your breathing and imagine that your third eye is opening. Tell yourself that you are attuned to your intuition and that you can hear it loud and clear. Repeat your affirmations with every breath that is coming and exiting your body.

### What Role Does Intuition Play in Tarot Readings?

Your intuition will be your guide and compass in any given reading. For instance, your intuition will tell you which cards you should pick up and whether a card should be upright or reversed. More importantly, this powerful tool will add to your insight. The cards will communicate what they mean, but your intuition will give you depth to your understanding and interpretation.

# Sacred Space

Meditation is necessary, but it is not essential for tarot reading. It is a way to sharpen your intuition, but it does not prepare you for reading. There are other ways to prepare yourself for a reading, like grounding techniques. Grounding looks and feels different for everyone, but if you have not tried any grounding techniques before, then try multiple ones until you find one that works for you.

Take a walk in nature. Embrace the sun on your skin and observe how the plants glisten in the sun. When you are done with your walk, sit on the ground and touch any plants around you. Connect with the earth and take deep breaths. This clears your mind and calms your spirit. You can also swim or take a shower. Connecting with water cleanses you and grounds you.

Grounding feels like establishing a connection or planting yourself in something that is much greater than you. You will feel calm, relaxed, and refreshed when you are done.

### Reading Setup

Setting yourself and your environment up for a tarot reading is almost like a ritual. There are several tasks that you need to do before getting into the reading. You will learn how to build an environment that will allow a safe space for smooth and clear readings.

### Cleansing

Your space, deck, and self must be cleaned before you begin and end a reading. There are several tools that you can use to cleanse everything, but the best tool that you can use is sage. Sage can cleanse anything it meets, unlike crystals. While crystals can cleanse a deck, they cannot cleanse you. So, before reading tarot, use sage to cleanse your space, energy, and deck. When you end the reading, use sage again. Cleansing the space before and after the reading is crucial.

### Techniques

You can use various techniques before you begin reading the cards. Every reader has their own style, and eventually, you will have a style you are comfortable with.

Some readers tap or knock on the cards three times before they shuffle. The knock is seen as a way to cleanse and refresh the cards. It is like hitting the refresh icon on a frozen page. After the three knocks, the readers begin to shuffle. You can shuffle the cards however you like; you can shuffle a Tarot deck the same way you would shuffle any pack of cards. Some readers like to cut the deck and then shuffle, while others do not. Try both and see what you are comfortable with, shuffling-wise. Lastly, questions play an important role in Tarot reading. This means that your questions must be precise and clear before you lay out the cards.

You can ask questions the more you delve into the reading, so you do not have to limit yourself to one question per reading.

## Tarot and Symbolism

Intuition is one of many tools that you will use when interpreting the cards. Remember that Tarot cards are not just mundane pictures on paper. On the contrary, they are one of the most effective and precise divination tools that are available for human use. This is not to say that your intuition is not powerful enough to understand Tarot.

Imagine that you are learning a second language. As a student, you need to attune your ears to the language and its music. On your learning journey, you will eventually memorize its letters and understand basic sentence structure. The more you practice and dedicate enough time and effort, the more you will acquire knowledge and become fluent.

It will be helpful to always look at Tarot cards through the same lens. You are a student, and Tarot is a foreign language that piques your interest. This divination tool does not communicate through letters and sentences; it speaks to you through symbols. This means that you will need to understand each symbol alone, then understand how each symbol gives a different meaning when it is around another symbol.

For instance, picture yourself shuffling your deck, and the Sun card flies out of the deck. The Sun card signifies universal harmony that is coming into your life, a joyful new beginning, and entering a successful path. Pulling out this card in a one-card reading means that you are on your way to a happy beginning or a new joyful beginning is very close.

Now, let's say that you pulled the Sun card with the Tower card. The Tower means transformation through failure or painful events. These two cards are almost the complete opposite of each other. It might be disturbing to see these two cards together, but the closer you look, you will find that they are trying to tell you that you will receive a blessing in disguise.

In other words, the cards warn you not to dismiss your coming blessing because it will not look like a blessing at first but will serve you the more you give it time. This can look like losing a job – only to find yourself available for a much better opportunity or ending a relationship because the person you were involved with was not good for you.

You can use several methods to understand the different combinations you will see. This means that you must clearly understand the card's elements, numerology, keywords, court cards, and Major and Minor Arcana.

### 1. Elements

If you are familiar with astrology's four main elements, you will also easily understand their meaning in tarot readings. The Minor Arcana represents the four elements of fire, earth, air, and water. These elements hide behind certain symbols in Tarot. This means that you need to make a connection between a certain image and one of the elements.

- **Suit of Wands**

  The suit of Wands represents fire in Tarot. As an element, fire in Tarot signifies several ideas, so use your discernment when interpreting a suit of Wands card.

  The suit of wands signifies masculine energy. This means that the card refers to someone who operates from divine masculine energy. It also means Aries, Leo, and Sagittarius. The cards could refer to a person with significant fire energies in their astrological chart. This element also means strength, passion, creativity, drive, and ambition.

- **Suit of Pentacles**

  The suit of Pentacles represents the earth in Tarot. Earth, or Pentacles, symbolizes feminine energy. This suit could also signify someone with a Taurus, Virgo, or Capricorn placement.

  Think of material earthly items and goals when you see the suit of Pentacles. In other words, any Pentacles card could mean riches, authority, taxes, career path, high or low status, winning or losing money, beauty, or receiving a gift.

- **Suit of Swords**

  The suit of Swords represents air in Tarot. As an element, air represents masculine energy. The suit of Swords represents people with air energy, like Gemini, Libra, or Aquarius.

  The suit of Swords means communication, swift action or change, knowledge, innovation, social skills, flaky energy, intelligence, and intellect.

- **Suit of Cups**

  The suit of Cups represents water in Tarot. Like earth, water is feminine energy as well. This suit could be referring to individuals with a Cancer, Scorpio, or Pisces placement in their chart.

The suit of Cups means emotions, feelings, intuition, psychic abilities, deep knowing or knowledge, spirituality, fantasy, imagination, relationships, love, and connections.

**Application**

**Seven of Cups and Ten of Pentacles**

Possible meaning: You will receive many riches (Ten of Pentacles), but your imagination (Seven of Cups) is tricking you into thinking that you must tend to several things simultaneously. To manifest the Ten of Pentacles in your life, you must first focus on the Cups, then gradually tend to the rest later.

**Nine of Wands and Four of Swords**

Possible meaning: You are juggling many things at the moment (Nine of Wands). You are running out of strength and willpower at the moment. This is why you need to make time for rest, even if it does not feel possible at the moment (Four of Swords). Together, these two cards tell you this is the time to rest. You do not need to rest indefinitely, but you need to find short times in the day to rest, breathe, and relax.

**2. Numerology**

Numerology tells us that every number has a certain meaning. You can apply numerology to your interpretation of the cards. Every card in the Tarot deck has a number. The Major and Minor Arcana have a number on the top of the cards. The court cards do not have a number on top, but you can interpret them as the "number one."

- 0-3

  Meaning: new beginnings, new cycles, or early stages.

- 4-6

  Meaning: progress or in the middle of the cycle.

- 7-10

  Meaning: endings, mature stages, or at the end of the cycle.

Now, what if you get a Major Arcana with two digits? For instance, the moon card has "18" on top. One way to interpret two-digit numbers is to add them together, so 1 + 8= 9. What if you have the Hierophant and the two wands? Numerologically, you can add 5 and 2 together, and it will give you 7.

Remember that numerology is one part of your interpretation, do not solely depend on it for full interpretations.

### Application
### The Lovers and Two of Cups

The lover's card has "6" on top, and the two cups card has "2" Depending on the reading, you can add or interpret the numbers alone. For instance, adding the numbers will give you the number "8." This means that the relationship you are reading about is in a mature stage. These cards can also signify a union between two people. The Two of Cups card tells us that this union will be new for the Lovers. Meaning that the "2" will be a new beginning for the "6" on top of the Lovers card.

### The Moon and the Two of Wands

The Moon card has "18" on top, and the two of Wands card has "2." Add 1+8=9, then add 9+2= 11, then finally, add 1+1=2. These two cards together imply that anxiety and fears are hindering your progress in the world. This means that you are in a new stage in your life, but your fears are holding you back from your progress.

### 3. Keywords

When studying Tarot cards, you will find that each has a set of keywords. For instance, upright, the three of Cups card's keywords are friendship, celebration, and creativity. When this card is in reverse, its keywords change, so think isolation and alone time.

Every card has two sets of keywords, a set for the upright card and another for the reversed card. This means that you will need to study and memorize all of the keywords so that you understand the overall meaning.

### Application
### The High Priestess and the Seven of Swords

Together, these two cards mean that you must use your intuition to understand a situation or a person you are dealing with. Why? Let's break these cards down. The Seven of Swords signifies a situation is not what it seems. It signifies a person deceiving you or a situation where you need to act strategically. The High Priestess means intuition and sacred knowledge. The cards could also mean you must use logic and intuition when making your next move. Your question will determine what the cards mean.

### The Queen of Pentacles and Judgement

The Queen of Pentacles' keywords is a homely, motherly figure, representing security and practicality. The judgment's keywords are forgiveness, rebirth, judgment, and inner calling. The meaning of these two cards together will differ depending on the question asked. However, possible meanings could be that you are entering a new phase of your life that will be more secure and homely, or you need to be more motherly with yourself or others.

### 4. Court Cards

The court cards are the Page, Knight, Queen, and King. The court cards do not have any numbers on them, and the person on the card will be holding one item. For instance, the Queen of Cups holds one cup, and the Knight of Swords holds one sword. You can draw many inferences based on the arrangement that you have.

### Application

### The Queen of Wands and Page of Swords

These two cards describe a person with a lot of energy and determination. The page of Swords confirms that this person will be able to achieve the goals of the Queen of Wands.

### The Knight of Pentacles and Page of Cups

Together, these two cards describe a goal-oriented individual, and while this is a good trait that will aid him in his quest, he also needs to listen to his heart as he strives to attain this goal. It also warns the person to adjust his ever-changing mood because it can hinder his quest.

### 5. Major and Minor Arcana

Generally, the Major and Minor Arcana signify two different situations. Major Arcana describes a karmic situation, while Minor Arcana refers to a temporary situation. For instance, the Tower card means destruction and transformation, while the Six of Wands card means victory and self-confidence. These two cards signify a karmic event that will change you in this phase of your life.

### Application

### The Tower and the Six Wands:

The Tower is a karmic event, while the Six of Wands card refers to a temporary phase. Together these two cards are telling you that you will go through a needed transformation phase that you cannot stop. This transformation period might be painful at first. Still, you will come out victorious and a much more confident individual after it.

### The Devil and Ace of Pentacles

These two cards tell you that your negative narrative about yourself is getting in the way of new opportunities and creativity. The Devil refers to restriction and shadow self. The Ace of Pentacles symbolizes new opportunities and prosperity. If you see these two cards together, you are being told that your shadow self is getting in the way of your blessings. This means you need to do shadow work to receive the blessings meant for you.

### Ending a Reading Session

Every Tarot reading feels like a journey. When you are done reading for yourself, thank the cards and cleanse them with sage. Then cleanse yourself and your space. If you are reading for another person, then make sure that all of their questions are answered. Of course, if you feel drained, apologize to the person and tell them you will continue this reading later if you can. Proceed with cleansing yourself, the client, the space, and the cards after you end the reading session rest. Resting is vital here; you do not want to exhaust yourself by doing demanding activities after a tarot session.

# FAQ

### 1. Can I do multiple readings?

It depends on your energy levels. If you feel like you can do another reading, then proceed. However, you must cleanse your space, yourself, and your cards before you begin another reading.

### 2. Why do I need to cleanse everything before and after reading?

This is a highly spiritual activity. This means that while using your intuition, you are also dealing with multiple energies. The nature of these energies is irrelevant. Whether they are heavy or light, you need to cleanse your space, yourself, and your environment from this energy. Also, energies from a previous Tarot reading can mix with another, hence the importance of cleansing before and after reading.

### 3. What if my interpretation is wrong?

It is necessary to practice with yourself before reading for others. If you are reading for yourself and you are questioning your interpretations, then ask the cards for a confirmation card. If the card confirms what you understood, then you were not wrong. If you are wrong, reassemble the cards, cleanse, meditate, knock on the cards, and read again.

Tarot reading is a beautiful step in your spiritual journey. This is no mundane activity. Tarot readings will bless you with rich insight and deep knowledge. The more you practice, the sharper your intuition will be. The readings you do for yourself will answer any questions you have. Eventually, you will be able to read for others and help them receive answers they could not access. However, before you reach this stage, you must study and practice to have accurate readings. Good luck and happy Tarot readings!

# Chapter 6: 7 Key Card Spreads

Tarot card spreads are an incredibly powerful tool for gaining insight into any situation. Whether you are a beginner looking to learn the basics or an experienced reader wanting to explore a new type of spread, there is literally something for everyone. Knowing the different spreads available as a Tarot reader will help you understand the cards and their meanings better and help you interpret your readings more accurately. From an easy-to-learn one, two, and three-card spread to the classic Celtic cross, this chapter will have beginners and advanced readers well on their way to a great foundation for learning the Tarot.

## What Is a Tarot Card Spread?

A spread is a configuration of cards laid out across a table, floor, or another surface.

Each spread is unique, but most incorporate a variety of cards that are selected and placed in a specific order. Spreads can be simple, such as three cards in a line, or more complex, such as a ten-card layout. The purpose of a Tarot card spread is to offer insight into a particular situation or question. While a single card reading can give you a general sense of the energy surrounding a situation, a Tarot card spread allows you to explore the situation from various perspectives. The idea is to get a more in-depth look at the situation and reveal a better idea of what is coming up in the future.

In general, a Tarot spread will consist of one card laid face up in the middle of the spread and a number of cards laid out around it. The positions of the cards laid out around the other cards indicate how they are related to the central card. For example, a three-card spread might consist of the central card flanked by two other cards, with each of the other cards showing one possible outcome for the central card.

## Benefits of Tarot Card Spreads

While a single card can reveal valuable information, a card spread allows you to explore a situation from various perspectives.

- A single card can often be misleading or unclear. A card spread gives you more information
- Through a card spread, you'll have insight into the situation, your emotions, and the people involved
- A spread is a great foundation for learning how to read the Tarot by practicing
- It allows for a more in-depth analysis of the situation.
- It is easier to focus on one situation or question at a time when using a card spread
- A card spread can be for any situation or question

Even advanced readers should try out different spreads to see which ones they prefer. This helps you become more comfortable with the cards and become better at reading them and the situation you've been questioning. Once you have become more familiar with the cards, you will be able to use Tarot spreads to improve your understanding and the accuracy of your readings. Using a specific layout will also help you focus. This is because each different layout highlights different aspects of a reading that might otherwise not come across as clearly. For example, a relationship spread can point out both positive and negative aspects of the relationship.

## How Do Beginner Tarot Readers Get Started?

It is true that some Tarot readers choose to start with a different type of spread immediately. However, beginners should start with the one-card spread. Why? The purpose of a spread is to enlighten your mind about a situation or question that you have. The one-card spread is one of the most basic spreads, so it's perfect for newbies to practice on. Once you're comfortable with the one-card spread, you can start branching out and trying other arrangements. But for now, the one-card spread is also one of the easiest to understand and interpret. It's also a great way to learn about cards and their meanings. As you practice with one card, you'll start to recognize patterns and discover meanings that fit your situation best. You'll also start to see how the cards relate to each other and how their messages interact. Let's begin with the easiest spread first and work our way up to more advanced spreads. Having this knowledge will help you deal with multiple cards and their meanings more effectively.

## One Card Spread (Beginners)

One-card spreads provide you with an interpretation of a single card. Since it's one of the easiest spreads to understand and use, it's often a good place for beginner Tarot readers. For example, say you want to know what to do about a strained friendship. Then you ask a question regarding this situation and pick up a card. This card will be your answer.

### 1. One-Card Tarot Spread

The reading for a one-card spread is pretty straightforward.

1. Simply pull a card from the top of the deck pile, or shuffle the cards and take the first one that drops out.
2. Then, read the card and determine what it means.

For example, suppose you set the intention to draw relationship advice. In that case, the card you choose will signify that relationship reading for you.

### 2. Yes or No Spread

The Yes or No spread is a simple yet powerful way to get an answer to a specific issue. This spread requires only using a single Tarot card. An upright card means yes, while an upside-down card means no. To get the reading right, the trick is to ensure the deck has the same number of upright cards as upside-down cards.

1. First, focus on the question you want the cards to answer, keeping your mind clear, and then select a Tarot card.
2. Once the card is chosen, consider the card's symbolism and overall meaning. You can then interpret the card and its message concerning the question you asked.

## Three-Card Spreads (Easy)

The three-card spread is a very common spread. It's one of the easiest spreads to interpret and gives you a rich, detailed perspective. Because it's such a common spread, there are multiple variations. In fact, there are so many variations of the three-card spread that you could almost call it a choose-your-own-adventure type spread. You can use a three-card spread to focus on a specific situation, explore options, or do a general reading.

3 card spread.³⁸

### 3. Sequence Spread

These spreads follow a sequence of events, are used to point out conflict, and are spread in a linear style. Basically, you line up three cards next to each other. The types of reading you get from a sequence spread include:

- Situation – Obstacle - Outcome
- Situation – Obstacle - Advice
- Aspiration – Progress - Idea
- Your potential - Your path - You
- Partner – Relationship - You

These spreads will offer a deeper understanding of a situation than the one-card spread and help you explore the best ways to move forward. The way to read them is like this:

1. Going from left to right, turn over each of the cards.
2. As a whole, this spread indicates a suggested path or outcome.
3. Past-Present-Future Spread

The Past-Present-Future Tarot spread is a classic three-card spread that provides an overview of a person's life. This spread is an excellent choice for someone looking for a general idea of what is going on in their life. It can also be used to make decisions or to clarify a particular issue. The spread consists of three cards laid out in a row, with the first card representing the past, the second representing the present, and the third card representing the future.

1. To begin the spread, shuffle the cards and then lay them out in the three-card spread
2. Then focus on the first card (left to right), which represents the past. This card will shed light on the events and experiences that have led to the current situation.
3. The second card, representing the present, will reveal details about the current situation and how it will likely evolve.
4. The third card, representing the future, will give insight into what could happen if the current situation continues.

### 4. Seven-Card Spread: The Horseshoe (Easy-Advanced)

The Horseshoe spread is one any self-respecting Tarot reader should have in their arsenal. And luckily, it's one of the easiest to learn. When arranged, this spread looks exactly like a Horseshoe, hence the name. It works best for open-ended questions and uncomplicated readings.

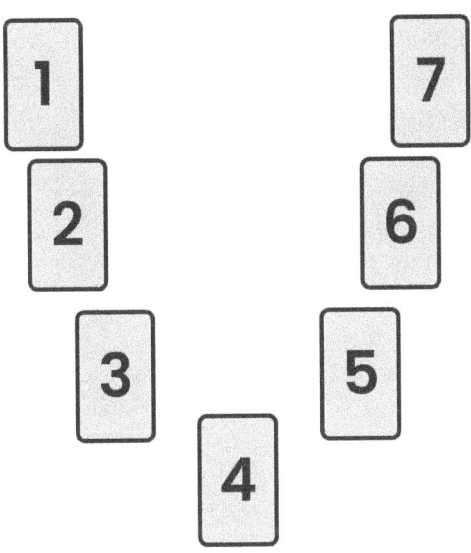

To begin the Horseshoe Tarot reading, determine what issue or question you want to answer. Focus on this as you shuffle the deck. In the next step, select seven cards and arrange them like this:

- **1st card:** Place this card down in front of you. This represents the past influences on the question or situation.
- **2nd card:** This card goes directly below the first card. It symbolizes the current circumstances surrounding the question or situation.
- **3rd card:** Then take a third card, and place it below the second card. This refers to internal conflicts of the subject of the reading.
- **4th card:** Place this card to the right of the third one. In some readings, this is the first card turned over because it symbolizes the client themselves.
- **5th card:** Now, place your fifth card to the right of the fourth card. This represents external factors such as other events or people.
- **6th card:** Place your sixth card directly above your first card. There is where you'll notice the horseshoe's shape beginning to form. This card shows the solution.
- **7th card:** Then lastly, the seventh card goes above the sixth one. This one symbolizes the outcome.

### 5. Ten Card Spread: The Celtic Cross (Intermediate)

The Celtic Cross spread is one of the most popular Tarot card spreads used today. It is a complex spread showing a comprehensive overview of a topic. This spread is made up of ten cards arranged in a cross pattern. The cards are laid out in a specific order to represent a particular question or theme. The layout is as follows:

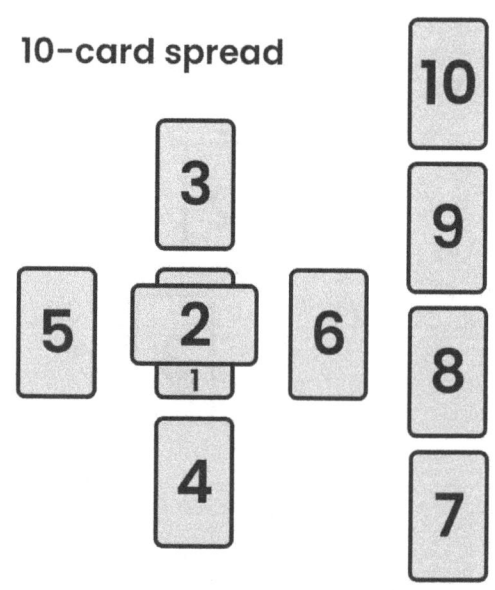

10-card spread

- **1st card:** Place your first card from the deck in the center. This card is typically interpreted as the main focus of the reading because it represents the subject of the reading.
- **2nd card:** Then place your second card directly (at an angle) on top of the first card. This one is interpreted as the main challenge or obstacle.
- **3rd card:** The third card goes to the left of cards one and two. This represents the past's influence.
- **4th card:** The fourth card goes to the right of cards one and two. This symbolizes the future's influence.
- **5th card:** The fifth card goes directly above the first card. This refers to goals and aspirations - things that the subject needs to achieve to resolve their issue.
- **6th card:** The sixth card goes directly below the first card and is placed to the left of the fifth. This card is interpreted as the unconscious fears associated with the situation.

By now, you should have a cross-like shape formed by one card on each side of the first card. Now arrange the cards like this:

- **7th card:** Place the seventh card to the bottom right, away from the cross shape. The card illustrates the subject's approach to overcoming adversity.
- **8th card:** The eighth card goes directly above the seventh card. This details the external influences or events that affect the reading as a whole.
- **9th card:** The ninth card goes directly above the eighth card. It symbolizes the hopes and fears of the subject.
- **10th card:** The last card is directly above the ninth card (the seventh to eighth cards should be in a vertical line). This last card represents the outcome of a situation.

## 6. Twelve Card Spread: The Zodiac Tarot Spread (Advanced)

This 12-card Tarot spread is based on the 12 signs of the zodiac and is designed to reveal key aspects of the questioner's life. Using the Tarot cards to explore the energies associated with each sign, start by gathering a set of Tarot cards and laying them out in a circle. Each card represents the twelve signs of the zodiac. There are a few variations of this spread, but the one here is the most basic form and best for beginners just starting. This spread works best with those already familiar with the zodiac signs. But anyone can learn to use it.

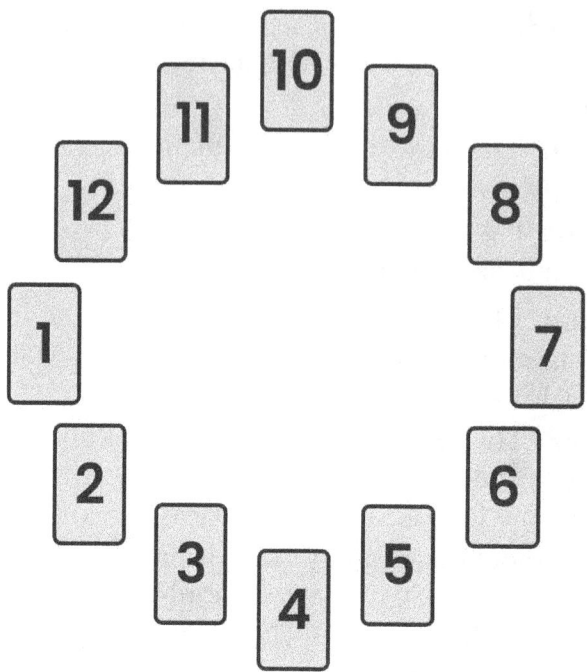

Shuffle the deck and place 12 cards in a circle. The first one is at the 9 o'clock position, with the rest following in an anti-clockwise position. This pattern should be followed until all twelve cards have been placed.

To interpret the Zodiac Tarot, you must know what each card symbolizes.

- **1st card:** Aries, The House of Aspirations - image
- **2nd card:** Taurus, The House of Security - the material
- **3rd card:** Gemini, The House of Thought - communication
- **4th card:** Cancer, The House of Emotion - family, home
- **5th card:** Leo, The House of Persona - creativity
- **6th card:** Virgo, The House of Detail - day-to-day habits
- **7th card:** Libra, The House of Balance - relationships
- **8th card:** Scorpio, The House of Intensity - secrets

- **9th card:** Sagittarius, The House of Philosophy - growth
- **10th card:** Capricorn, The House of Pragmatism - career
- **11th card:** Aquarius, The House of Originality - community
- **12th card:** Pisces, The House of Intuition - the unconscious mind

Turn each card over one by one, and consider how each card relates to the sign it represents.

Then, interpret the whole spread. Think about how each card in the spread relates to the other cards. How do they combine to form a cohesive message?

## Tips for Reading Spreads

When it comes to reading Tarot spreads, a few tips guarantee a successful experience. To begin with, make sure that you select a spread appropriate for the issue or questions being addressed. There are many different types of spreads available. And another great thing about Tarot reading is that it is possible to repurpose the spreads to your desired question or situation. Other things to remember:

- Remember that Tarot card spreads do not guarantee a specific outcome. Although the cards can shed light on a situation, interpretation is always possible
- Always work with a clear mind. Before you read the cards, make sure that you are in a calm and clear state of mind
- Always shuffle the cards before a reading. Be sure to shuffle the cards to attune and connect with the deck
- Pay attention to how the cards feel. This is because each card has a specific energy associated with it. By paying attention to how the cards feel, the meaning of the card will become clearer to you
- Remember that you will get what you put into reading. If you are reading with the intention of receiving guidance, the cards will give you guidance. If you are reading with the intention of receiving insight, the cards will give you insight
- Consider the connection between each card. A complete reading involves studying the spread as a whole. Don't be afraid to think outside the box.

# Adapting Tarot Spreads

Altering a Tarot spread to your needs is crucial to reading Tarot cards. By doing this, you can concentrate on certain aspects of your life while expanding your knowledge about different areas. Whether you are a beginner or an experienced Tarot reader, here are a few ways to change a spread for the best results.

1. Determine the purpose of the spread. Is it for guidance, insight, or a simple yes or no answer? Knowing your purpose will help you choose the right cards and how many cards to use.

2. Don't be afraid to open your mind to the multitude of possibilities each card brings as you draw them into the overall reading. Consider the different meanings of each card and choose the ones that will best answer your question or offer guidance.

3. Decide how many cards to use. A spread with too few cards won't give enough detail, while a spread with too many cards will be overwhelming, especially for beginners. Consider your purpose and the situation's complexity to determine the right number of cards to use.

4. Play around with the placement of the cards. Changing the order in which you turn the cards over will benefit you as you learn, give you a different perspective, and reveal more information. Think about how the cards relate to each other and how the order of the cards reveals more than what is simply in front of you. Get inventive with your imagination.

5. Finally, take your time. Don't rush the process of modifying a Tarot spread to your particular needs. Take the time to consider the different aspects of your life and how the cards might relate to each other. This will help you learn more in the long run.

Learning Tarot card spreads is a great way to understand yourself better and develop a higher awareness of yourself and your surroundings. They reveal powerful guidance and support in all areas of your life, from relationships to careers to spiritual growth. By starting with the essentials, you'll tap into your intuition and uncover hidden aspects of yourself and others while you learn. Through this journey of self-discovery, you'll be clearer on your life path and confidently make decisions. Tarot card spreads also create a sense of connection with the divine, allowing you to receive messages from the universe and access deeper levels of your inner wisdom. And if you are interested in Tarot reading as a career, education is the key. Understanding the different spreads gives you a highly sought-after skill many of your clients will appreciate. Learning key Tarot card spreads will also increase your knowledge and confidence in your abilities. Just remember to take your time. Tarot reading is an exciting and fulfilling process, and ensuring you learn correctly will only benefit you in the future.

# Chapter 7: Spreads for Love and Self-Care

One of the worst feelings in the world is having your love life stuck in limbo with no knowledge of the future and no one to guide you forward. Fortunately, Tarot cards provide a comprehensive interpretation of your love life. Many people are attracted to Tarot reading with questions about love. The powerful messages revealed in a reading can shed light on the present, past, and future romantic events in your life. Questions like "What does my future with my partner look like?" Will I ever find my soulmate?" or "What can I expect for the future of my marriage?" are the most common in Tarot love readings. The meanings and implications of the cards are interpreted by considering the meaningful interactions between the cards. Therefore, considering the order and position of each card is an essential step in interpreting the readings. So, the intuitive insight from Tarot readings can give you all the advice you need to move forward, whether you're in love, out of love, or hoping to find love.

## General Love Spread

**Difficulty Rating:** ★★☆☆

This General Love Spread is one you can practice regularly to keep track of how your love life is faring. It's a pretty simple yet insightful spread that doesn't require a lot of experience or practice to get accurate results. You can reflect on your current relationship, including your partner's and your own feelings. Consisting of just three Tarot cards, the layout is simple to interpret and explain. You can perform this reading as often as once a day to tune into the energy of the day. Once you get into the habit of performing this reading daily, you can identify any problems, conflicts, disputes, and concerns before they escalate or plan dates and surprises for the most suitable times.

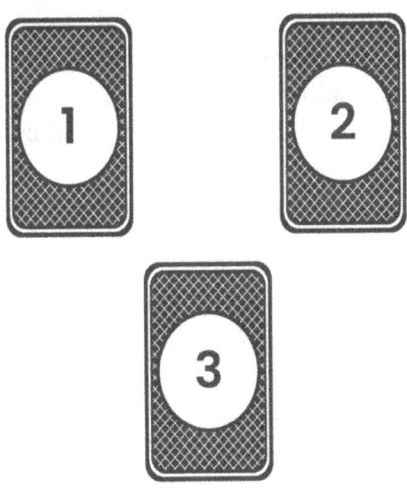

### Casting the Cards

- Place the first card in the left corner, in a vertical position. This card represents you in the relationship.
- Place the second card in the right corner, in a vertical position. This position represents your partner in the relationship.
- Place the third card between the first two cards in a horizontal position. This card represents the current state of the relationship.

### Interpretation

The first card represents your feelings, including happiness, sadness, thoughts, insecurities, or doubts regarding your relationship and partner. Similarly, the second card represents your partner's feelings about the relationship. Finally, the third card signifies your current state or potential together. For instance, imagine you've placed the following cards in order:

1. The Temperance
2. The High Priestess
3. The Hierophant

According to the Temperance card, your personality is reflected in the relationship as secure and balanced. If you're single, this would be a good time to welcome a new romantic interest into your life. If you're in a relationship, this card suggests that the relationship helps you become a better version of yourself by constantly evolving, developing, and accessing new parts of yourself. On the other hand, the High Priestess reflects your partner's creativity, spirituality, and, most of all, love for your relationship. Finally, the third card, the Hierophant, signifies a structured union. The appearance of this card could suggest a literal marriage, or it could reflect that the relationship is publicly recognized and will last a long time.

## Past, Present, and Future Love Spread

**Difficulty Rating:** ★★★☆☆

This Tarot spread connects your relationship's past, present, and future situations and helps you understand where it is headed. This is an ideal spread to read when you want to figure out what lies ahead for you and your partner. It also helps you understand how events in the past relating to your romantic life connect with and influence your present and future love lives. The present moment card will give you insight into how you're balancing past and future circumstances. The future card will predict how your relationship will move forward. If the future card is something you're not hoping for, you can always change the predicted outcome in your present moment because it's not set in stone.

1. Past
2. Present
3. Future

### Casting the Cards

- Place the first card in the left corner, in a vertical position. This card represents your own self in the relationship.
- Place the second card in the right corner, in a vertical position. This position represents your partner in the relationship.
- Place the third card between the first two cards in a horizontal position. This card represents the current state of the relationship.
- Place the fourth card below the third card in a vertical position. This card represents your past.
- Finally, place the fifth card above the third card, in a vertical position, in alignment with the fourth card. This card represents your future.

### Interpretation

Like the interpretation described above, the first card reflects your feelings about the relationship and your partner. The second card suggests your partner's feelings about you, and the third represents your relationship's current potential. The fourth card shows how your past connects with your present and how it has shaped it. Finally, the fifth card will predict how your future will be shaped in connection with your present and past circumstances. Let's take the same example for the first three cards, while the remaining two can be assumed to be:

1. The Temperance
2. The High Priestess
3. The Hierophant
4. Ace of Wands
5. Three of Pentacles

Imagine that this is a person you have just met. In this case, the first three cards might make little sense to you. After all, why has the Hierophant card shown up for someone you haven't known for long? However, once you consider the past and future cards, the Tarot spread will start making a lot more sense. For instance, the Ace could reflect that this person is someone you've had feelings for longer than you think, and now, they have started to develop into something stronger. The Three of Pentacles card can hint at a future collaboration with this person. A reading like this can also suggest that you will be excellent creative partners with this person but not necessarily romantic partners, which means you would be better off as friends.

## Stay or Go Spread

**Difficulty Rating:** ★★★☆☆

Although it's difficult to consider letting go of a person, even when things aren't working, doing so may be for your own good. However, letting go of them is especially challenging if you truly care about them. Deciding whether to stay in a relationship or end it is a serious decision that has life-altering consequences for both of you.

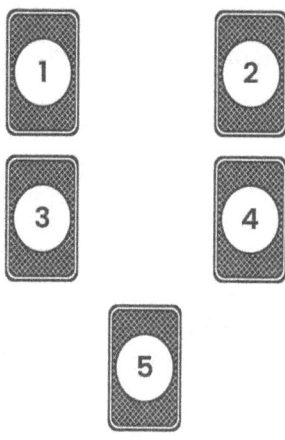

1 = Future with my partner if I remain in the relationship
2 = My future if I remain in this relationship
3 = Future with my partner if I leave it
4 = My future if I leave this relationship
5 = Advice to consider

Making a decision about whether you should continue or end a relationship is not easy. There will always be consequences either way for you and your partner. Luckily, what you can do is turn to Tarot reading to help guide you and make the decision-making process much easier. This Stay or Go Spread will provide insight regarding either future or the path you decide to take.

### Casting the Cards

- Place the first card in the left corner, in a vertical position. This card will suggest changes that need to be made if you stay.
- Place the second card next to the first one in a vertical direction. This card will represent how you must act if you stay in the relationship.
- The third card should be placed next to the second one but slightly above it. This card will help you decide whether to stay in or leave the relationship.
- Place the fourth card to the right of the third card, in a vertical position and in alignment with the first and second cards. This card will define the purpose of the relationship if you decide to leave.
- Place the fifth card in the right corner, in a vertical position. This card will suggest how you must let go of the relationship.

### Interpretation

The first card represents the changes needed to make your relationship whole again. This will give you the insight you need regarding changing your and your partner's attitudes concerning the relationship. The second card will suggest how you need to act with your partner once you decide to stay. The third card will help you make your final decision regarding the relationship. The fourth card will explain the relationship's purpose or meaning if you decide to leave. This will give you closure and let you move on from the relationship in a calm way. Finally, the fifth card will suggest how you move on from the relationship. Let's consider an example reading with the following tarot cards:

1. The Hanged Man
2. The Queen of Swords
3. The Lovers
4. Seven of Pentacles
5. Three of Cups

Before observing any of the other four Tarot cards in this spread, you will need to consider the third card, as it will help you make your final decision. In this case, the third card, the Lovers, suggests that your relationship will go much deeper. This means that you can decide to stay. Next, consider the cards placed on the left side of the spread. The

Hanged Man suggests that you must stop being so passive and accommodating. You need to bring this change to your relationship to improve it. The Queen of Sword advises you to speak your heart and be assertive to better navigate your relationship. If the third card signaled your decision to be "no," the Seven of Pentacles would reflect that your relationship taught you patience. The Three of Cups would suggest that you celebrate the good friendships you have and leave the past behind.

## Love Compatibility Spread

**Difficulty Rating:** ★★★☆☆

This spread is a variation of the five-card Tarot Love Spread, which helps you determine if you are compatible with a new romantic interest. This is a fun spread to try out when you start dating someone new, as it will not only help determine your compatibility but also reveal the intentions you and your partner have for each other. As a result, both of you will have an open understanding of each other's desires, leaving little to no room for misunderstandings or unmet expectations. This reading will also show your likes, dislikes, common interests, and similarities. All of these factors will be helpful when starting a new relationship.

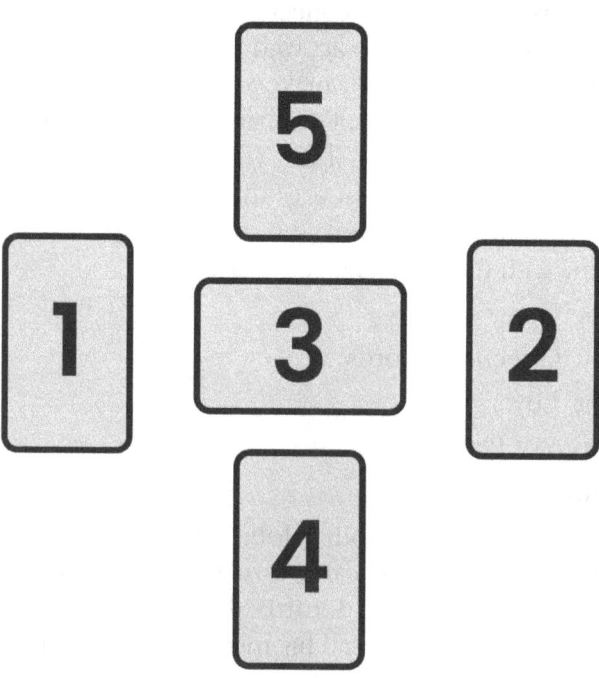

### Casting the Cards

- Place the first card at the left-hand corner of the table in a vertical position. This card represents your feelings about the person.
- Place the second card at the right side of the spread, again, in a vertical direction. This card will represent your partner's feelings towards you.
- The third card will need to be placed between the first two cards in a horizontal position. This card will determine the dominant feature of the relationship.
- The fourth card should be placed below the third card in a vertical direction. This card will represent the challenges or conflicts that you might face in the relationship.
- Finally, the fifth card should be aligned with the fourth card, right above the third (center) card. This card will indicate the potential of the relationship.

### Interpretation

In this Love Tarot Spread, the first and second cards represent your feelings and your partner's feelings, respectively. They will tell you how well you and your partner are connected or aligned. The third card may be the most important one in this spread. It will dictate the tone or major characteristic of your relationship. Sometimes the third card might not reflect the overall relationship status. Still, something unique might be influencing it at the moment, which might be reflected. The fourth and fifth cards provide insight into the relationship dynamics. They will predict any conflicting situations or the strong potential of your relationship. The overall reading will also provide insight into how this relationship might affect your life. Let's consider an example with the following tarot spread:

- The Three of Wands
- The King of Pentacles
- The Six of Pentacles
- The Five of Wands
- The Two of Pentacles

The Three of Wands indicates that your feelings have a strong base but require effort to deepen. The King of Pentacles shows how stable and secure your partner feels in your relationship. The Six of Pentacles represents union, which is also the main theme of your relationship. Moving further, the Five of Wands suggests that the relationship will have opposing ideas, and neither party will be willing to compromise. Finally, the fifth card, the Two of Pentacles, suggests that a balance should be maintained for the relationship to succeed, and each of you needs to adapt to the other's expectations.

## The Soul Mate Spread

**Difficulty Rating:** ★★★★☆

Many people believe in the concept of soulmates. Some believe we can have multiple soulmates, while others argue that one person can only have a single soulmate for life. Wherever your beliefs are, this Soulmate Tarot Spread can help determine whether a person is or isn't your soulmate. This helpful spread can help you get the guidance you seek and identify if someone really is your soulmate. The difficulty level of this spread is a bit higher than others because of the complicated interpretation it requires.

### Casting the Cards

- Place the first card at the top-middle of the spread in a vertical position. This card represents the characteristics of your soulmate.
- Place the second card in the right corner, in a vertical position. This position represents your partner in the relationship.
- Place the third card between the first two cards in a horizontal position. This card represents the current state of the relationship.

### Interpretation

The first card reflects an aspect of your soulmate's personality. It can either point towards physical or emotional characteristics in your soulmate. The second card represents the circumstances in which you will meet. These could include a trend, a personality, or an external force. The third card will suggest the actions you can take to make the meeting possible. The fourth card depicts any obstacles possibly preventing your meeting with your soulmate. The final position represents an overall assessment of the reading. This is something you should be mindful of.

1. The Queen of Wands
2. The Two of Swords

3. The Six of Pentacles
4. The Sun
5. The Seven of Cups

Your soulmate is a master of social skills. They have good social aptitude, determination, and confidence. Although their social skills come easily to them, this is not the true source of their power. The situation in which you meet your soulmate may involve you having to make a difficult decision. The Two of Swords reflects that you should pay attention to your heart and your intuition in this situation. The Six of Pentacles card suggests being selfless and kind during this situation. Make a just decision, no matter how hard it is. When making this decision, remember that the roles could be reversed. The Sun reflects that there will be no obstacles in your meeting with your soulmate. An inverted Seven of Cups card indicates that caution is to be exercised when making this decision; often, things aren't as they seem.

Although all relationships bring you a share of happiness and joy, the right one will prove to be immensely rewarding. At the same time, relationships also bring conflict, sorrow, hardship, and transformation. All relationships can be considered to be a journey of love. No matter your stage, it's crucial to put in the effort and make time for your loved one. Uncertainties are also a common part of relationships, whether you're at the beginning of a new relationship or deeply in love with a person. Various Tarot spreads can help reveal important lessons, courses of action, and useful insight that can be used to improve your relationship. By tuning into the wisdom of these Tarot spreads, you will have full access to knowledge about the best course of action moving forward.

# Chapter 8: Spreads for Spiritual Development

Like the previous one, this chapter also lists several helpful Tarot spreads, this time for spiritual development. Developing a close relationship between your intuition, the cards, and yourself can be incredibly beneficial for spiritual growth and personal development. It is another form of self-care that inspires you to learn about yourself. The best thing about spreads for spiritual development is that you can include them regardless of your religious and cultural background. The Tarot card layouts described here have different difficulty ratings, so you can decide whether they're suitable for your experience level.

## Tree of Life Spread

**Difficulty Rating:** ★★★★☆

The Tree of Life is a powerful symbol in several belief systems, from Norse mythology to Kabbalah to Celtic practices. The following spread has taken inspiration from all of these religious traditions, yet it enables you to incorporate parts of your own spiritual beliefs. It's also great for self-discovery and reflecting on what you can do to change your life.

# Tree of Life Spread

### Casting the Cards

This spread uses 10 cards which you will arrange in a tree shape. Cards 1-4 should be laid down in the middle, cards 5-7 on the left, and cards 8-10 on the right. The stem of the Tree of Life reflects your personality. The branches to the left represent your connection to nature and the universe. The branches towards the right symbolize your future and the path you'll be taking based on your current actions. More specifically:

- The first card represents your spiritual state
- The second card denotes your traits and personality
- The third card indicates knowledge hidden in your subconscious
- The fourth card represents your home and your relationship with your family
- The fifth card reveals your connection to your ancestors
- The sixth card symbolizes the link you have to your past

- The seventh card reveals your connection to all the other realms
- The eighth card symbolizes the wisdom you've gathered throughout your life
- The ninth card indicates personal growth and spiritual development
- The tenth card embodies renewal and rebirth

**Interpretation**

As an example, let's say that you have the following cards in your spread:

1. Wheel of Fortune
2. King of Swords
3. Queen of Cups
4. Ace of Pentacles
5. The Fool
6. The Hierophant
7. The Moon
8. Eight of Wands
9. The World
10. Seven of Wands

Your first card is the Wheel of Fortune. It symbolizes things you can't control. Since it came up in the spirituality position, you can see it as a reminder that you'll need to trust the universe that your spiritual development will be favorable. You need to allow the wheel to take you wherever it wants to because it's moving in the right direction. Pulling the King of Swords in your personal card means you're a strong person who thinks logically. At the same time, drawing the Queen of Cups in your subconscious card suggests that deep down, you're a sensitive individual; you are just repressing this part of yourself. You've received the Ace of Pentacles in your family card, which indicates that you value financial stability. Then, you have The Fool in your ancestral card. This card is about taking a huge leap into the unknown. If you're in a situation where you need to take risks, this card encourages you to do so. The past card revealed The Hierophant, a card denoting traditions and conventions you've lived by in the past. Consider whether they still affect you in your present life. Your connection with the other worlds unveiled The Moon, indicating that you're probably confused about what lies in those realms. The Eight of Wands symbolizes progress, and if you have received the wisdom card, you're on the right path toward personal growth. This is reinforced by your growth card, which is The World. In this context, this card indicates that you have achieved much of what you have been working on for so long. And finally, you've received the Seven of Wands in your rebirth card. According to this, you're ready to take on your next challenge. As long as you stand your ground and learn how to overcome even larger challenges, you'll persevere whatever you put your mind to.

While it's not recommended to alter the structure of the spread (as it would defy the purpose of the Tree of Life layout), you can make a few modifications when reading it. For example, after reading cards 1-4, you can start interpreting cards 5-7, except in reverse order. Instead of your connection to the ancestors, you can learn first about your link to the other realms. This can come in handy if you want to establish a relationship with spiritual guides other than your ancestors.

## Flower of Life Spread

**Difficulty Rating:** ★☆☆☆☆

The Flower of Life is another ancient symbol related to nature. It stands for growth and fertility, as the flower produces the seeds that give life. In Tarot, this symbol is linked to spiritual growth and self-empowerment through the renewal of one's life. The Flower of Life layout is a fantastic option for answering non-specific questions. While the ancient symbol has 19 overlapping circles, the Tarot spread is much simpler than that. It uses only six cards, each revealing specific influences in your life. They are as follows:

- The first card relates to the current energies ruling your mind, body, and spirit
- The second card indicates any external influences affecting future outcomes
- The third card denotes current challenges and things you need to let go of
- The fourth card reveals the strengths and personality traits you need to cultivate
- The fifth card symbolizes messages you've received from your spiritual guides

- The sixth card highlights expected future outcomes based on current actions

## Casting the Cards

To cast the cards, place a round object in the middle of the space you're working on (altar, table, floor, etc.). This can be a plate, a piece of cloth, or anything that has a round shape. Arrange the six cards around it. Start by placing the first one on top of the round object. Moving clockwise, place the second and third cards on the right, the fourth one in the middle, and the fifth and sixth cards to the left of the object.

## Interpretation

Let's say you've pulled the following cards:

1. Knight of Wands
2. The Judgment
3. Five of Cups
4. King of Swords
5. The Lovers
6. Nine of Pentacles

Revealing the Knight of Wands as your current energy card indicates you're ready for action. You're buzzing with positive energy and are prepared to take on any challenge. The Judgment card in the external influences position reveals that you feel judged by others for your actions, thoughts, and emotions. The Five of Cups indicates that you may even turn to self-pity due to the reactions you perceive from those around you. However, the next card, the King of Swords, highlights that you should focus on disciplining yourself to leave these thoughts behind instead of giving in to your grievances. Your spiritual guides are telling you to move on to work on establishing new and stronger relationships based on your values and mutual acceptance. And finally, the Nine of Pentacles reveals that by working hard towards your spiritual and personal goals, you'll be able to enjoy the fruits of your labor.

While the spread works best with general inquiries, you can also ask it open-ended questions. However, you should avoid asking specific questions. For example, instead of asking about the best way to move on from a relationship, you should ask what you can do to empower yourself. The answers will help you achieve your goal – even if they aren't specific – because through growth and empowerment, you can achieve everything.

# Connect with Your Spirit Guides Spread

**Difficulty Rating:** ★★☆☆☆

A spiritual guide can be any spirit from this world or any other realm. The most common spirit guides are ancestral spirits, guardian angels, animal spirits, higher beings, and living spirit guides. Whoever your guides are, the following Tarot spread will help you form a meaningful connection with them, so you can work with them in the future.

**Casting the Cards**

Place the five cards face-down, forming a star. Begin by placing the first card at the top of the star, the second on the top left position, and the third on the top right. The fourth card goes into the bottom left position. The fifth one should make up the bottom right corner of the star. Here is what the cards represent:

- The first card symbolizes who the spirit is and what can they help you with
- The second card reveals the message your guide has for you at this moment
- The third card hints at certain parts of the message you might be afraid to hear
- The fourth card shows you how to be more open to your guides in the future
- The fifth card indicates how the information you've learned will contribute to your spiritual growth

**Interpretation**

Let's say you've pulled the following cards:

1. Queen of Cups.
2. Six of Swords.
3. The Magician.
4. The Justice.
5. Queen of Wands.

The Queen of Cups in the first position indicates that your spirit guide is a nurturing and compassionate person with whom you had a close relationship. It could be a family member you've always admired for their serene nature, and they're there to impart their wisdom regarding patience. Maybe you're too impatient to reach your goals and end up self-sabotaging your success. The Six of Swords shows that you're in a transitional period, which means you'll soon leave behind whatever is making you impatient. The Magician in this position suggests that you're afraid that leaving behind parts of yourself will hold you back from manifesting your desires. The Justice card indicates that if you're clear in communicating your intention to your guides, they can provide you with more straightforward messages in the future. The Queen of Wands signals that you can establish a meaningful relationship with your spirit guides by being determined to form a strong connection with them. Consequently, you will trust their messages even more in the future.

Connecting with your spirit guides is a very intuitive practice. Trusting your gut feelings during Tarot readings will go a long way in accurately interpreting messages. Take your time and consider what each card represents to you and your connection with your spiritual guide.

## Spiritual Gift Spread

**Difficulty Rating:** ★★★☆☆

Each person has spiritual gifts, but not everyone is aware of theirs. You may be holding back from acknowledging your aptitudes because of fear, anxiety, or uncertainty. Or, you might not understand how to explore your spiritual skill or express them. This spread is designed to reveal your spiritual gifts and help you learn a little more about them. While this spread seems like a simple 5-card layout, it requires some introspective awareness, which takes some practice to develop.

**Casting the Cards**

Start by laying down the first card in the center, face down. Place the second one over it and the third one to its left. The fourth card goes below the first one, and the fifth one is on its right side. Here is what they represent:

- The first card symbolizes yourself and your relation to your spiritual gifts
- The second card reveals talents you are aware of
- The third card identifies any issues that are holding you back from using your gifts
- The fourth card denotes gifts you haven't acknowledged yet

- The fifth card hints at practices that can help you embrace your gifts

**Interpretation**

Let's say you've revealed the following cards:

1. The Hanged Man
2. Four of Wands
3. Eight of Wands
4. The Empress
5. Six of Wands

The Hanged Man in the central position indicates that you're feeling powerless in your situation. Perhaps you've sensed your spiritual gifts emerging but aren't sure how to deal with them. The Four of Wands signals that you're probably talented in creating a stable, loving environment for your loved ones. The Eight of Wands symbolizes impatience. In this instance, it means that even if you become aware of your gifts, you want them to develop instantly. Pulling the Empress into the fourth position means you aren't fully aware of how much you can do with your talents. The Six of Wands indicates that you can work toward expressing your gifts by seeing yourself as successful in the role that allows using them.

You can look at the theme you see emerging from the cards. For instance, you've seen three Wands cards in the example above, which means a lot of activity. It indicates that to successfully connect with your gifts, you might need to slow down and let things happen as they're naturally supposed to.

## Shadow Work Spread

**Difficulty Rating:** ★★★☆☆

Many people put things they're afraid of, ashamed of, or embarrassed about to the back of their minds. Instead of confronting these issues, they're repressing them, creating a shadow self, which prevents them from reaching their full potential. However, facing your shadows can actually help dispel their harmful effects and enable you to create a more positive self-image. This layout is perfect for exploring the depths of shadow work, the practice of revealing one's shadows and working through them. Many shadow spreads exist, but this one is chosen for its simplicity. Yet, through five cards, it can provide a comprehensive insight into yourself.

**Casting the Cards**

Start by placing the first card face down in the middle of the space in front of you. Next, place the second card directly under it and the third one over it. Place the fourth card on the left side of the first and the fifth one on its right side. Here is what these cards represent:

- The first card will serve as a tool for identifying a shadow trait
- The second card will reveal why you held onto this shadow trait
- The third card symbolizes a hard truth you need to learn about the trait
- The fourth card hints at possible practical applications of the trait
- The fifth card reveals how to take care of yourself while exploring your shadow trait

**Interpretation**

Let's say you've revealed the following cards:

1. The Emperor
2. The Devil
3. Four of Cups
4. Eight of Wands
5. Queen of Swords

Having The Emperor in the shadow trait position indicates that your traits are structure and control. Perhaps you're trying to manage things you can't control, or maybe you have trouble establishing your authority. The Devil in the second position reveals that you've probably held onto this shadow trait because you're addicted to relying on it. The Four of Cups indicates that you've distanced yourself from your true desires due to your controlling ways. Because of this, you're now discontent with your life and are contemplating how to break the cycle. The Eight of Wands, in this context, reveals that you can still use your shadow trait in a challenging situation. When time is of the essence, your ability to control a situation and make quick decisions can go a long way toward success. Finally, the Queen of Swords tells you that the best way to take care of yourself during shadow work is to always be perceptive and open-minded.

For the best results, spend a little time with each card as you pull them and lay them out in the spread. While you're free to stay with the meanings mentioned here, make sure to take a few seconds to contemplate what each card means to you at that moment.

# A Few Honorable Mentions

# The Soul Activation Spread

Difficulty Rating: ★★☆☆☆

### Casting and Interpretation

After choosing a card to depict you, lay it on the table. You'll place the following 3 cards below it, from left to right. Here is what all the card in this spread represents:

- The first card indicates the energy you want to manifest into the world
- The second card denotes past influences on your energy and future outcomes
- The third card represents who you are in the current time
- The fourth card will activate your spiritual growth

# New Year's Tarot Spread

Difficulty Rating: ★★★★☆

### Casting and Interpretation

You'll need eight cards. You'll lay the first three cards out face down, from left to right. Leaving a little space under them, place the fourth card in the middle and the fifth one on top of it in a horizontal position. The next card goes to the left of the fourth, while the seventh is placed on the right. Place the eighth card between the first and second rows in the middle. Here is what they mean:

- The first card depicts the biggest lessons you've learned during the year
- The second card highlights your most prominent achievement throughout the year
- The third card symbolizes the things you let go of last year
- The fourth card hints at experiences you can expect in the coming year

- The fifth card reveals major obstacles you'll encounter in the coming year
- The sixth card shows what you will focus on during the new year
- The seventh card transmits advice you should listen to for the coming year
- The eighth card reveals how your transition from the past year to the new one will be

## Making Tough Choices Spread

**Difficulty Rating:** ★☆☆☆☆

### Casting and Interpretation

In this simple spread, you'll lay the first three cards in a horizontal line, beginning from at the top and moving down. Then, you'll place the fourth card on the left and the fifth one on the right side of the second card. Here is how to interpret this layout:

- The first card is linked to your motivation and how whatever inspires you affects your decision
- The second card symbolizes the ideal outcome you expect to achieve under the current circumstances
- The third card reflects your core values and principles and how they affect your decision
- The fourth card shows one of the likely outcomes of following your current path
- The fifth card demonstrates another of the likely outcomes of following your current path

# Chapter 9: Spreads for Work and Career

This chapter brings you spreads for work and career. While a few layouts in this chapter focus strictly on professional life, others have slightly different purposes. For example, you'll find spreads for establishing a work-life balance, getting along with your coworkers, and finding out what makes you happy career-wise.

## Work-Life Balance Spread

**Difficulty Rating:** ★★☆☆☆

Finding the precarious balance between your professional and personal life is tricky. It comes down to your priorities, which must be set and adhered to. Otherwise, habits from one aspect of your life will seep into the other and vice versa. The following spread for a work-life balance acts as a bridge between situations, tasks, and relationships you prioritize in your life and what you're overlooking. It helps you understand what's out of balance, so you can resolve the issue.

### Casting the Cards

Start by placing the first card on the upper part of the far left side of your table. On the lower part of the right side, you'll put the second card. Position the third card on the right side of the first one, just a little lower. Lastly, place the fourth one under the third one on the left side of the fourth card. Here is what these cards symbolize:

- The first card represents what you're currently prioritizing
- The second card shows what you need to pay more attention to
- The third card reveals why you prioritize certain things
- The fourth card tells you why you need to focus on things that require your attention

**Interpretation**

Let's say you've drawn the following cards:

1. Seven of Cups
2. Ace of Wands
3. Eight of Pentacles
4. The Tower

Seven of Cups in the first position indicates that you don't have priorities because you're trying to excel in all areas of life. However, because you have so many goals and tasks, you can't focus on a single one sufficiently to make it a priority. This card typically refers to one's personal life, showing that you have so many things going for you personally that it affects your professional development. This message is underlined by the Ace of Wands, telling you that what you need to prioritize is singling out one thing to focus on. This should be a smaller goal or task, so it wouldn't interfere with the rest of them. The Eight of Pentacles symbolizes that you're looking at the bigger picture. You're chasing big dreams, so you can't focus on smaller goals. The Tower tells you that the reason you can't focus on one thing is that you're afraid. You fear that by doing so, you'll neglect the other areas, and consequently, you'll fail to realize your biggest dreams.

While the first two cards are easy to decipher, the third and fourth need more attention. Make sure to look at their relationship to see if you can see any patterns. Sometimes there will be an evident conflict between the two reasons, which you can explore through additional readings.

## Finding Opportunities Spread

**Difficulty Rating:** ★★★★☆

Whether you're unemployed or are looking to move on from your current position, job hunting can be challenging. Finding a suitable job prospect is hard enough, and getting through the interview and winning is even more problematic. This spread is designed to help you with the first part of that task, finding job opportunities suitable for your skills and preferences.

## Casting the Cards

Lay down the first of the six cards you'll use face down in the middle of your table in a horizontal position. Place the second one on top of it in a vertical position. Visualizing a square around these two cards, place the third card in the top left corner of the square. Finish the spread by placing the fourth one in the top right corner, the fifth one in the bottom left corner, and the sixth card in the bottom right corner of your imaginary square. Here is what these cards represent:

- The first card points to your attitude regarding your job search, including preconceived expectations and their effects
- The second card shows the biggest obstacle you must overcome to find the best career opportunities
- The third card highlights your skills, including the ones you can offer to your employer, the ones you're using, and the ones you've overlooked
- The fourth card represents your secret weapon, something that helps distinguish you from all other applicants
- The fifth card tells you something you have to understand about your motivations before being successful in your job hunting
- The sixth card offers advice going forward in terms of what you should focus on and where you should spend your energy

## Interpretation

Let's say you've revealed the following cards:
1. The Chariot
2. The Wheel of Fortune
3. King of Wands
4. Two of Cups
5. King of Swords
6. Knight of Pentacles

Drawing the Chariot in the first position indicates that you believe that finding the right job will give you more control over your life. While this may be partially true, you're too focused on this aspect and forget that you're supposed to be looking for something fulfilling. The Wheel of

Fortune tells you that your biggest obstacle will be fate. If you didn't get a job you were hoping to get, there is probably a reason for that. The King of Wands in your skills position is a good indicator of excellent leadership skills. You can persevere and work hard for your goals, not to mention to look at the big picture. You'll always do a thorough job, which is a desirable skill. Make sure to emphasize this skill to potential employers during your next job hunt. The Two of Cups is the partnership card, which means your secret weapon is being a good team worker. The King of Swords indicates that you need a little more discipline. When job hunting, you should listen to your head instead of following your heart. Your final advice comes from the Knight of Pentacles. This card symbolizes perseverance which means that by putting in the hard work, you'll be able to land your dream job.

This spread can reveal any obstacles that might obstruct your view of the best opportunities. When drawing on the cards, focus on identifying the internal barrier or issues that may arise later. For example, landing your dream job can mean relocating your entire family.

## Finding Your Life Goals Spread

Difficulty Rating: ★★☆☆☆

If you want to learn more about your life's goals, this general-purpose spread is a valuable tool. Whether you're feeling stuck, undetermined about your position, or happy where you are currently in life, this layout will help you identify whether you're on the right track toward reaching your goals.

### Casting the Cards

You'll need six cards. You'll place the first three in a row, face down, from left to right. Lay the fourth and fifth cards above the first row. The sixth one goes above the second row. Here is what these cards symbolize:

- The first card reveals why you choose certain job roles and what purpose they serve in your life
- The second card highlights the primary motivating forces that inspire you to do your best
- The third card indicates the responsibilities you're willing to take on, whether they're in the job description or not
- The fourth card tells you what projects you like to work on and what sort of work environment you prefer

- The fifth card shows the potential rewards you're interested in gaining from your new job, spiritually, financially, or otherwise
- The sixth card hints at where you are heading and what your future goals can bring to you

**Interpretation**

Let's say you've cast the following spread:

1. Three of Pentacles
2. Page of Swords
3. Four of Swords
4. Three of Cups
5. Ten of Wands
6. The World

If you've drawn the Three of Pentacles in your first position, you choose jobs where you will collaborate with others. You value teamwork and will always do your best to work well with your teammates. The Page of Swords in the second position means you're also driven by curiosity and have plenty of mental energy to work productively, even under stress. Four of Swords is a card that, in this instance, tells you that you're willing to take on tasks that require a lot of analysis and patience. You have the Three of Cups in your preferred environment position. It indicates that you prefer a close-knit community-type of work culture where you can form long-lasting friendships with your coworkers. The Ten of Wands suggest that your reward will be spiritual fulfillment. And while the rewards will come with even more responsibilities, the World card indicates that what waits for you at the end of the journey will be more than worth all your hard work.

No matter your results, it's always worth considering the bigger picture. Make sure to always look at all of the cards in your spread to see if there is a connection between them.

## Career Shift Spread

**Difficulty Rating:** ★☆☆☆☆

Some say it's always a good idea to leave a job when you're still satisfied with your position. However, deciding when to change careers is never easy. The following spread will clarify where you are in terms of your professional goals, allowing you to decide whether you should look for a new opportunity.

**Casting the Cards**

You'll lay three of the seven cards in a horizontal line, starting from the left. Place the fourth and fifth cards under the first and second one in a second horizontal line. Lastly, put the sixth and the seventh card under the fourth and fourth ones, forming a third row. Here is what these seven cards symbolize:

- The first three cards represent options you should be contemplating for your next career
- The fourth card highlights your possible future career, letting you see how it looks
- The fifth card tells you what to do to have that career
- The sixth hints at things you need to let go of to move toward the desired career
- The seventh card indicates how your life will change when you start that career

**Interpretation**

Let's say you've revealed the following cards:

1. The Hermit
2. The Death
3. Knight of Wands
4. Five of Wands
5. Seven of Cups
6. Eight of Swords
7. King of Pentacles

The Hermit indicates that one of your future jobs could be related to work that requires using your intuition. The Death card denotes that another one of your prospects could be in a dynamic environment. The Knight of Wands supports this indicating that you're in for plenty of action in your new job. The Five of Wands tells you you're looking into plenty of competition in your future career. The Seven of Cups reveals that you'll need to look into your purposes and the choices you are willing to make to find your dream job. The Eight of Swords indicates that you're prone to self-victimization, and if you want to succeed, you'll need to stop this behavior. And lastly, the King of Pentacles shows you that landing your dream job means abundance and prosperity in your future.

One of the modifications you can make is to use only one card to reveal your future career. This way, the rest of your answers will be more specific. Or, you can do separate readings for all three suggested options after an initial one to clarify the answers you got on the last four positions.

## Career Direction Spread

**Difficulty Rating:** ★☆☆☆☆

If you aren't sure whether your current career is heading in the right direction, this spread can clarify this matter. It will help you learn whether you'll still find this role fulfilling in the future or whether you should look into something more rewarding.

### Casting the Cards

Place the first card face down in the middle of the space and arrange cards 2-5 around it. Start from the left corner and work in the clockwise direction filling each corner of an imaginary square. Here is what these cards mean for career direction:

- The first card represents your current career as a whole
- The second card hints at steps you'll need to take in your career
- The third card tells you how you'll know that you're taking the right steps
- The fourth card denotes the skills you'll need further in your career
- The fifth card shows what you can do to further your career

### Interpretation

Let's say you've drawn the following cards:

1. The Fool
2. The Hanged Man
3. Six of Wands
4. Knight of Swords
5. Knight of Pentacles

As the first card of the Major Arcana, the Fool symbolizes the beginning of your journey. Your career is just beginning, and you still have a lot of learning to do. The Hanged Man indicates that your chosen profession will require some sacrifices. The Six of Wands is a card of success, which means you'll soon taste your first victory. When you do, you'll know you're on the right path. The Knight of Swords in the fourth position denotes that you'll make good use of your skills, like pursuing your goals, proving points, and letting others see things from your perspective. The Knight of Pentacles reassures you that the best way to further your career is to work hard for your goals.

You can modify your inquiry by being more specific with your question. For example, in the last question, you can ask whether taking a particular step will further your career.

## You and Your Coworkers Spread

**Difficulty Rating:** ★☆☆☆

Sometimes it's difficult to get along with coworkers because you don't understand each other. This can affect your productivity and result in strained relationships at the workplace. This spread will help you uncover more about your coworkers and learn how to get along with them. The key is understanding your and your coworkers' needs and finding a bridge between them.

### Casting the Cards

Draw three cards and lay them on the table, face down. Here is what they represent:

- The first card symbolizes your coworker's needs
- The second card denotes your own needs
- The third card illustrates an overlap between the two needs as a way of finding common ground

### Interpretation

Let's say you've revealed the following cards:

1. Eight of Wands
2. Ten of Wands
3. Two of Pentacles

Drawing the Eight of Wands as your coworker's card means that they probably like to resolve everything through quick actions. And while they're only focusing on finishing the job as soon as possible, you see it as unnecessary rushing that can lead to mistakes. The Ten of Wands in the second position shows that you prefer to work hard, even if you have to do everything yourself. In fact, you may even take on a task from your coworker because you want to ensure it gets done accurately. The Two of Pentacles is a card linked to time management and adaptability. It could indicate that you should see your coworkers' traits as strengths instead of weaknesses. Perhaps it's good that they don't over-analyze things as you do. Otherwise, work would take much longer to get done.

Besides the images on the cards, you should also look at the bigger picture they represent. For example, here you have two Wands cards, which means you have two people with excellent work ethics and committed to their job. However, the two Wands are turning away from each other, which means they aren't on the same wavelength. The good news is you have a common ground, which isn't always the case. For example, the first two cards could stand in opposition, indicating that you and your coworker have nothing in common personality-wise. You can also alter this spread to include more than one coworker if needed. You'll just add a card for each coworker's needs.

# A Few Honorable Mentions

# Judgement Spread for Career Evaluation

**Difficulty Rating:** ★★☆☆☆

### Casting and Interpretation

You'll lay the first card on the left side of your space and the second one under it, leaving a little space between them. The remaining cards (3-6) go next to the first two on the right side, starting around the middle of both cards. Here is what the cards in this layout mean:

- The first card represents past mistakes you've made in your professional life
- The second card denotes the successes you achieved in your professional life
- The third card indicates the lessons you've learned from the successes and the failures
- The fourth card shows new information you're learning or acknowledging
- The fifth card symbolizes your transformation after receiving the information

- The sixth card highlights the changes your transformation will bring to your professional life

# The Emperor Spread for Standing up for Yourself

**Difficulty Rating:** ★★★★☆

### Casting and Interpretation

Start by placing the first card on the right side of the table. Put the second one on the left side of the first one and the third on the right side of the first one. The fourth card goes under the first one, between the second and third cards. Cards five and six (using the same format as cards one and four) go on the left side, next to the second one. Here is what these six cards mean:

- The first card offers clarity on why you feel that you lack control in your workplace
- The second card shows what you have control over and how to use this control
- The third card symbolizes everything that's out of your control
- The fourth card represents everything you should stop tolerating and say no to moving forward
- The fifth card highlights everything you need to keep doing and pay more attention to
- The sixth card indicates everything that brings you joy and fulfillment in your career

# Chapter 10: Create Your Own Tarot Spreads

This chapter is a step-by-step guide to help you create personalized Tarot spreads that align with your reading style. Here, you'll learn how to develop original positions, orders, and layouts based on a single question, problem, or goal. You'll also understand how to modify a ready-made Tarot spread if you don't want to create one from scratch.

## Step 1: Know the Question and Pinpoint Your Goal

There are two factors you must consider when creating a tarot spread. You won't be able to create a spread without knowing the question needing to be asked and identifying the goal of the spread. Whether you're creating a spread for yourself for a client reading, it's a lot easier if you understand the question since it fulfills a current need. Determining the goal, however, could be more challenging. Goals hint at long-term, future needs. They shape our motives, actions, and even the questions that we have at the moment. The problem with identifying our goals is that they're not always acknowledged on a conscious level. People who have low levels of self-awareness might struggle to identify their goals. Many people find it hard to name their deepest desires. Fortunately, there are Tarot readings that can provide guidance on the subject.

Suppose you are doing the reading for someone else. In that case, you might not have a solid understanding of their goals and desires, especially if they feel uncomfortable sharing this type of information with you. In that case, you'll have to make do with the background knowledge you have. Try to use it to get a general idea of what they desire most in life. If they are dealing with a certain problem, be empathetic and try to relate to how they're feeling. Learning as much as possible about their desires and problems ensures that your reading is heading in the right direction and offers satisfactory information. Ultimately, the reading should provide a sense of clarity and even enlightenment.

If you're creating the Tarot spread for yourself, then this step will likely be easy. Take a moment to introspect and reflect on your past and current experience. You can also practice positive visualization to get a better grip on your goals and the future that you want for yourself. Now that you know the purpose of your Tarot spread, you can move on to the next step.

## Step 2: Develop the Positions for Your Tarot Spread

This step requires a little effort and focus on your side. Creating Tarot spreads and developing positions requires you to take on the role of an investigator. Use all the information you have about the person you are reading to or the relevant information you have about yourself to come up with specific, narrowed-down questions. It helps to know what type of answers you need for clarity. Once you have the questions you need, break each one down into three distinct parts. The whole point of a Tarot reading is to tell a story or paint a picture in which you or your client act as the main characters.

Like any other story, your Tarot reading must illustrate the situation, the environment, the circumstances, the main problem, possible challenges, and the solution. This structure would make the reading more interesting and compelling and ensure that you deliver a comprehensive and detailed message. This is why you must have sufficient information about current affairs and any behaviors, personality traits, and past events that might influence the outcome.

## Step 3: Expand Your Horizons

You might feel very confused about where to start, what type of information to gather, and how to ensure you receive all the answers you need. Your questions lay the foundation for the Tarot spread you'll be building. You need to pinpoint the pieces of context that will affect your reading. Too much knowledge can be confusing and might cause you to lose sight of the purpose of the spread. Too little information would result in an unsatisfactory reading.

The following questions will give you ideas regarding what to ask yourself or your client. When working with instruments of divination, you should always follow your intuition. Don't let these examples limit you; use them as sources of inspiration and tweak them and add to them as needed.

Ask yourself:

- What type of information am I seeking?
- What do I need to know at the moment?
- What do I think is hidden or concealed?
- Who is involved or plays a role in the situation I'm in?
- Where or who can I turn to for guidance and help?
- Where do I stand in my journey?
- What are the things that I can't control in life?
- How is my environment?
- How am I seen by others?
- What are the potential opportunities, and where can I find them?
- How am I approaching and dealing with the problem at hand?

## Step 4: Target the Problem

When going through the questions mentioned in the previous step, you might be surprised by how easy it is to grasp the problem. However, you must remind yourself that what's easy to express and put into words is often very shallow and lacks depth or meaning. As you explore your personal journey and work with more clients, you'll find that the easily-articulated things often distract from the bigger picture – and the things that truly matter.

For instance, if you're going through a rough patch with your partner, you might think that your recurrent arguments, recent traumatic experiences, or other external factors are the main reasons behind the tension between you. You might not necessarily realize that something within either (or both) of you might be the root of the problem. Perhaps you have unresolved trauma, an unhealthy coping mechanism, or a detrimental behavioral pattern. For instance, an argument about whose turn it is to do the laundry might be really about your inability to communicate or clearly express your needs.

To be able to target the root problem, you should ask yourself (or your client) the following questions:

- Is there anything blocking you/me from moving forward?
- Are there any obstacles standing in our/my way?
- What are the things that you/I can change in your/my life?
- What is the biggest challenge you're/I'm facing at the moment?
- What is your/my deepest desire?
- What do you/I truly wish for?
- What is your/my greatest goal in life?
- What are things that you/I need to work on?
- Is there anything that you/I wish to develop in yourself/myself?
- What are some things that would bring you/me joy and happiness?
- What are your/my strengths and weaknesses?

## Step 5: Come Up with a Solution

Tarot can be a very powerful tool if you set reasonable expectations for your readings. If you're expecting your cards to tell the future or uncover the unknown, then you'll be setting yourself up for disappointment. Tarot is a way to get clarity and guidance on your current position in life and the actions you can take to control your future and the circumstances at hand. It can give you insight into which road to take and the confidence you need to make things right. It is an empowering tool that allows you to focus on what you can do instead of lamenting your problems. If you're giving the reading to someone else, make sure to know their expectations and correct any misconceptions they might have about Tarot readings.

Otherwise, they won't be satisfied with what you have to offer.

To find the solution to your problem, ask yourself the following questions:

- What can I do to alleviate the problem?
- Is there something that I need to redirect my attention to?
- How can I make the best use of potential opportunities?
- Is there something holding me back that I need to let go of?
- Is there a lesson that I need to learn?
- Where is this road leading me?
- Where or who can I turn to for helpful advice?
- What can help me overcome this roadblock?

## Step 6: Create a Tarot Spread Layout

You don't need to ask yourself or your client all the questions mentioned above. Once you've decided on the most relevant and helpful ones and got the answers you need, you should start painting your picture. Think about the direction the story will take and the order in which all your answers will come up. Picture what your story will look like. Follow your intuition when creating your spread, laying them out in the shape of anything relevant to your spread's theme. A cross is a popular shape for anyone with many decisions to make. If you value balance or want to learn about both the positive and negative sides of the question or issue at hand, you can lay out your cards symmetrically. Many Tarot readings find that symmetrical and balanced layouts allow them to do better readings.

Remember, however, that while visual layouts can yield better-quality readings, they don't matter much. If you wish to give a quick reading, you can simply lay down the cards beside each other. If you want to know something in particular, you need to think about the order in which you lay down your cards; this is more important than their visual representation. The story you tell is the most important aspect of your Tarot spread, and the story is the reading itself. At its most basic level, a story is told by explaining the current circumstances, introducing the problem, and then coming up with a resolution.

## Step 7: Give Your Tarot Spread a Try

To use your spread effectively, you must ensure that all the details tie in seamlessly. This is considered the most exciting part of the process, especially for those in design and user experience testing. In this step, you need to determine which parts are working, which ones are off, and how you can improve the overall quality of the spread. You'll find that the more readings you do with your Tarot spread, the more knowledge and ideas you'll learn regarding how to fix it up and refine it until you're satisfied.

## Modify a Ready-Made Spread

There are many great Tarot spreads out there. You've probably encountered several you like but thought they were lacking in one area or another. Instead of creating your own spread from the start, you can modify it to suit you. Tweaking a spread doesn't have to be tedious; you can simply modify it by changing the numbering or the positional meaning. Some Tarot readers even argue that if you modify an existing spread, you create a brand-new one.

Modifying a Tarot spread requires you to make small changes that align with your reading style, your (or your client's) questions, and personal beliefs. You can modify a spread in several ways. Still, before you make any changes, you must think about its initial purpose. Analyze the cards' layout and positions and whether the spread successfully meets its initial purpose. If you're certain that it doesn't suit you, take a moment to ponder how it would better suit you.

The following are some points to consider:

- *The focus of the spread.* Do you need to change the intrinsic purpose of the spread so it suits your needs more effectively?

- *The positional meanings of the deck.* Do the positions of the cards align with your questions? Do you think they'll give you the answers you're looking for? Do you wish to add or remove some positions?

- *The layout of the spread.* Does the layout look right to you? Does it fit the changes you made in the positions? Would it be easier to read the cards if you changed the layout?

- *The number of cards.* According to your reading style, are the cards present too many or too few to give you an effective reading?
- *Techniques.* Which reading technique can you use to enrich your reading and make the best use of your spread?

Now that you know everything you need to know about creating Tarot spreads from scratch, you are ready to personalize the whole reading experience. Learning how to modify Tarot spreads so they fit your personal style makes you better at giving readings overall.

# Conclusion

From a simple parlor game to one of the most effective divinatory tools, Tarot has come a long way since its introduction to society. That said, the most popular decks used today are still based on the ones created during the late 19th and early 20th centuries. The Rider-Waite deck, in particular, is heavily featured among the modern variants, and this book has introduced you to its structure and symbolism. You've learned about the meanings of the 22 Major Arcana cards and the 56 Minor Arcana cards and how you can apply them to the different aspects of your life.

You've also read about the importance of tuning in to your intuition when connecting with your deck. Tarot readings can teach you many things about yourself and how to persevere in life, but you'll need to form a connection with them. For beginners, steps like choosing the right deck, holding each card in your hands, and contemplating its meaning can go a long way in learning how to do Tarot readings. Because, more often than not, the messages you receive through the cards will be tied to what the cards mean to you rather than their general symbolism.

After providing plenty of advice on reading and interpreting the cards using your intuition, you were introduced to the most popular general spreads. The layouts with the lower number of cards are perfect for practicing basic Tarot reading skills. These will be the ideal stepping stone for more elaborate work. Mastering these will also give you the opportunity to seek answers to problems you encounter in different areas of life. Cards with higher numbers can offer you generalized advice on various matters.

If you want to explore specific matters in more depth, you can use the spreads provided. For example, you can do a reading for finding or strengthening love, self-care, and spiritual growth. These are all crucial elements of keeping your life balanced, but you can't forget about your professional life either. Feel free to use the spread supplied in the penultimate chapter to find answers for career development.

Another splendid option for finding answers to specific issues is to create your own spreads. Developing original positions based on your requirements, goals, or questions requires actively engaging your intuition from start to finish. This takes a lot of practice and time to master, but the final results will definitely be worth it. The best way to start is to modify existing spreads and see what your gut tells you about the new layouts and the results they deliver. Later on, you can decide whether you want to come up with entirely new spreads or stick to doing original ones. Either way, good luck on your Tarot journey and finding the answers you seek for your life.

If you enjoyed this book, I'd greatly appreciate a review on Amazon because it helps me to create more books that people want. It would mean a lot to hear from you.

**To leave a review:**
1. Open your camera app.
2. Point your mobile device at the QR code.
3. The review page will appear in your web browser.

*Thanks for your support!*

# Here's another book by Mari Silva that you might like

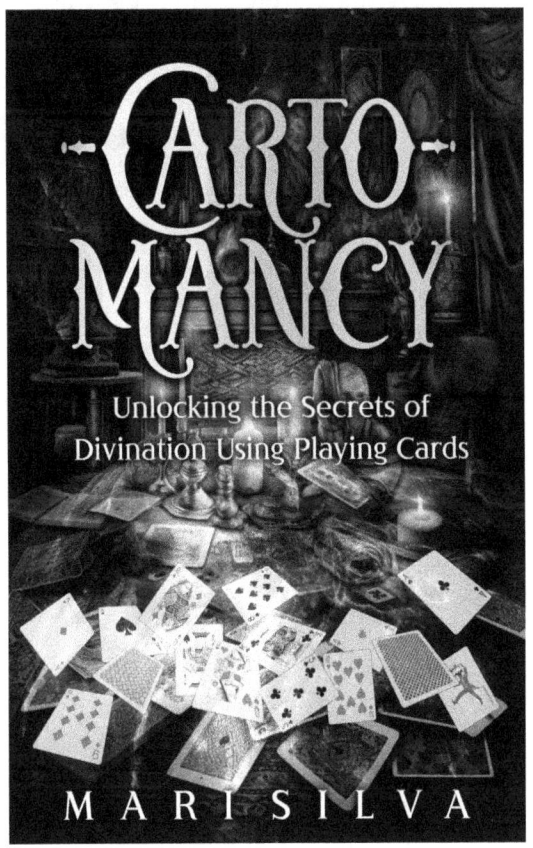

# Your Free Gift
# (only available for a limited time)

Thanks for getting this book! If you want to learn more about various spirituality topics, then join Mari Silva's community and get a free guided meditation MP3 for awakening your third eye. This guided meditation mp3 is designed to open and strengthen ones third eye so you can experience a higher state of consciousness. Simply visit the link below the image to get started.

https://spiritualityspot.com/meditation

Or, Scan the QR code!

# References

2019. "Get to Know Your New Deck with the Tarot Deck Interview Spread." Little Red Tarot. February 6, 2019. https://littleredtarot.com/tarot-deck-interview-spread/.

"Tarot 101 - How to Connect with Your New Tarot Deck." 2021. Labyrinthos. August 2, 2021. https://labyrinthos.co/blogs/learn-tarot-with-labyrinthos-academy/tarot-101-how-to-connect-with-your-new-tarot-deck.

8 of Cups meaning love, career, health, upright & reversed. (2021, March 15). MyPandit. https://www.mypandit.com/tarot/minor-arcana/suit-of-cups/eight-of-cups/

9 of Wands meaning, feelings, upright & reversed – guide. (2021, March 24). MyPandit. https://www.mypandit.com/tarot/minor-arcana/suit-of-wands/nine-of-wands/

A New Year's Tarot Spread - Lessons from the Past and Looking Ahead. (2018, December 30). Labyrinthos. https://labyrinthos.co/blogs/learn-tarot-with-labyrinthos-academy/a-new-years-tarot-spread-lessons-from-the-past-and-looking-ahead

Ace of Cups Tarot card meanings. (2011, December 22). Biddy Tarot. https://www.biddytarot.com/tarot-card-meanings/minor-arcana/suit-of-cups/ace-of-cups/

Ace of Cups. (n.d.). Astrotalk. https://astrotalk.com/tarot/ace-of-cups

Ace of Pentacles Tarot card meaning, love, feelings, upright & reversed. (2021, March 19). MyPandit. https://www.mypandit.com/tarot/minor-arcana/suit-of-pentacles/ace-of-pentacles/

Ace of Pentacles Tarot card meanings. (2011, December 22). Biddy Tarot. https://www.biddytarot.com/tarot-card-meanings/minor-arcana/suit-of-pentacles/ace-of-pentacles/

Ace of swords meaning, love, feelings, upright & reversed – guide. (2021, April 27). MyPandit. https://www.mypandit.com/tarot/minor-arcana/suit-of-swords/ace-of-swords/

Ace of Swords Tarot card meanings. (2011, December 22). Biddy Tarot. https://www.biddytarot.com/tarot-card-meanings/minor-arcana/suit-of-swords/ace-of-swords/

Ace of Wands Tarot card meanings. (2011, December 22). Biddy Tarot. https://www.biddytarot.com/tarot-card-meanings/minor-arcana/suit-of-wands/ace-of-wands/

Ace of Wands Tarot guide: Meaning, upright & reversed. (n.d.). Mypandit.com. https://www.mypandit.com/amp/tarot/minor-arcana/suit-of-wands/ace-of-wands/

Alecha Tarot Journals. (2019a). King of swords: Dotted tarot journal, dot grid journal, journaling diary, dotted writing log, tarot lovers dot grid notebook sheets to write inspirations, lists, goals. Independently Published.

Alecha Tarot Journals. (2019b). King of wands: Dotted tarot journal, dot grid journal, journaling diary, dotted writing log, tarot lovers dot grid notebook sheets to write inspirations, lists, goals. Independently Published.

Alecha Tarot Journals. (2019c). Page of pentacles: Dotted tarot journal, dot grid journal, journaling diary, dotted writing log, tarot lovers dot grid notebook sheets to write inspirations, lists, goals. Independently Published.

Amber, B., Lou, Linda, B., & Wille. (2022, November 6). 47 Best Tarot Card Decks Listed and Ranked. A Little Spark of Joy. https://www.alittlesparkofjoy.com/tarot-decks/

Astrotalk - online astrology horoscope prediction by astrologer. (n.d.). Astrotalk. https://astrotalk.com/tarot/knight-of-cups

Beth. (2014, June 18). Fool's journey: Create your own tarot spread. Autostraddle. https://www.autostraddle.com/fools-journey-create-your-own-tarot-spread-241932/

Beth. 2016. "Fool's Journey: Get to Know Your New Tarot Deck with the Interview Spread." Autostraddle. July 27, 2016. https://www.autostraddle.com/fools-journey-get-to-know-your-new-tarot-deck-with-the-interview-spread-346310/.

Breckon, I. (2010). Knight of swords. Old Street Publishing.

Bretton, J. D. (2017). Eight of cups: The tarot trilogy, book two. Splintered Sky Publishing.

Casey, N. (2022). King of cups: A dark college bully romance. Independently Published.

Chalex Tarot Journals. (2019a). Ace of swords: Tarot diary log book, record and interpret readings, daily draw journal. Independently Published.

Chalex Tarot Journals. (2019b). King of pentacles: Tarot journal diary log book, record and interpret readings, 3 tarot card spread journal. Independently Published.

Chalex Tarot Journals. (2019c). Knight of pentacles: Tarot diary log book, record and interpret readings, daily draw journal. Independently Published.

Chalex Tarot Journals. (2019d). Ten of pentacles: Tarot diary log book, record and interpret readings, daily draw journal. Independently Published.

Chalex Tarot Journals. (2019e). Ten of swords: Tarot diary log book, record and interpret readings, daily draw journal. Independently Published.

Chariot Tarot card meaning, upright, reversed & guide. (2021, April 5). MyPandit. https://www.mypandit.com/tarot/major-arcana/chariot/

Connect with Your Spirit Guides Tarot Spread. (2021, October 8). California Psychics. https://www.californiapsychics.com/blog/psychic-tools-abilities/tarot-oracle-and-angel-cards/connect-spirit-guides-tarot-spread.html

Crawford, C. (2019, December 21). How to Use a 3 Card Tarot Spread For Self Care —. The Self-Care Emporium. https://theselfcareemporium.com/blog/tarot-card-spread-self-care

Crawford, C. (2021, March 2). Finding work/life balance tarot spread —. The Self-Care Emporium. https://theselfcareemporium.com/blog/finding-worklife-balance-tarot-spread

DailyTarotGirl. (2012, July 22). Sharing Your Gifts ~ 5 Card Tarot Spread. Daily Tarot Girl. https://daily-tarot-girl.com/tarot-card-spreads/sharing-your-gifts-5-card-tarot-spread/

daysinspired. (2021, April 22). 5 Shadow Work Tarot Spreads to Uncover and Integrate Your Shadow Self. Days Inspired. https://daysinspired.com/shadow-work-tarot-spreads/

Death tarot card – meaning, upright-reverse, love, health & guide. (2021, March 19). MyPandit. https://www.mypandit.com/tarot/major-arcana/death/

Death Tarot card meanings. (2011, December 22). Biddy Tarot. https://www.biddytarot.com/tarot-card-meanings/major-arcana/death/

Death. (n.d.). Astrotalk. https://astrotalk.com/tarot/death

Devil Tarot card meaning, love, upright & reverse - complete guide. (2021, March 29). MyPandit. https://www.mypandit.com/tarot/major-arcana/devil/

Divination, E. L. (2019, November 18). Career Direction Tarot Spread. Emerald Lotus Divination. https://www.emeraldlotusdivination.com/blog/careerdirection

DLC Tarot Journals. (2019a). Five of swords: Tarot diary log book, record and interpret readings, daily draw journal. Independently Published.

DLC Tarot Journals. (2019b). Five of wands: Tarot journal diary log book, record and interpret readings, 3 tarot card spread journal. Independently Published.

DLC Tarot Journals. (2019c). Four of swords: Tarot diary log book, record and interpret readings, daily draw journal. Independently Published.

DLC Tarot Journals. (2019d). Nine of swords: Tarot journal diary log book, record and interpret readings, 3 tarot card spread journal. Independently Published.

DLC Tarot Journals. (2019e). Page of wands: Tarot diary log book, record and interpret readings, daily draw journal. Independently Published.

DLC Tarot Journals. (2019f). Queen of pentacles: Tarot diary log book, record and interpret readings, daily draw journal. Independently Published.

DLC Tarot Notebooks. (2019a). Ace of pentacles: Tarot diary log book, record and interpret readings, lined notebook journal for tarot lovers. Independently Published.

DLC Tarot Notebooks. (2019b). Ace of wands: Tarot diary log book, record and interpret readings, lined notebook journal for tarot lovers. Independently Published.

DLC Tarot Notebooks. (2019c). Eight of pentacles: Tarot diary log book, record and interpret readings, lined notebook journal for tarot lovers. Independently Published.

DLC Tarot Notebooks. (2019d). Eight of wands: Tarot diary log book, record and interpret readings, lined notebook journal for tarot lovers. Independently Published.

DLC Tarot Notebooks. (2019e). Four of pentacles: Tarot diary log book, record and interpret readings, lined notebook journal for tarot lovers. Independently Published.

DLC Tarot Notebooks. (2019f). Four of wands: Tarot diary log book, record and interpret readings, lined notebook journal for tarot lovers. Independently Published.

DLC Tarot Notebooks. (2019g). Knight of wands: Tarot diary log book, record and interpret readings, lined notebook journal for tarot lovers. Independently Published.

DLC Tarot Notebooks. (2019h). Nine of pentacles: Tarot diary log book, record and interpret readings, lined notebook journal for tarot lovers. Independently Published.

DLC Tarot Notebooks. (2019i). Nine of wands: Tarot diary log book, record and interpret readings, lined notebook journal for tarot lovers. Independently Published.

DLC Tarot Notebooks. (2019j). Page of cups: Tarot diary log book, record and interpret readings, lined notebook journal for tarot lovers. Independently Published.

DLC Tarot Notebooks. (2019k). Seven of pentacles: Tarot diary log book, record and interpret readings, lined notebook journal for tarot lovers. Independently Published.

DLC Tarot Notebooks. (2019l). Seven of wands: Tarot diary log book, record and interpret readings, lined notebook journal for tarot lovers. Independently Published.

DLC Tarot Notebooks. (2019m). Six of pentacles: Tarot diary log book, record and interpret readings, lined notebook journal for tarot lovers. Independently Published.

DLC Tarot Notebooks. (2019n). Six of wands: Tarot diary log book, record and interpret readings, lined notebook journal for tarot lovers. Independently Published.

DLC Tarot Notebooks. (2019o). Ten of wands: Tarot diary log book, record and interpret readings, lined notebook journal for tarot lovers. Independently Published.

DLC Tarot Notebooks. (2019p). Three of pentacles: Tarot diary log book, record and interpret readings, lined notebook journal for tarot lovers. Independently Published.

DLC Tarot Notebooks. (2019q). Three of swords: Tarot diary log book, record and interpret readings, lined notebook journal for tarot lovers. Independently Published.

DLC Tarot Notebooks. (2019r). Three of wands: Tarot diary log book, record and interpret readings, lined notebook journal for tarot lovers. Independently Published.

DLC Tarot Notebooks. (2019s). Two of pentacles: Tarot diary log book, record and interpret readings, lined notebook journal for tarot lovers. Independently Published.

DLC Tarot Notebooks. (2019t). Two of wands: Tarot diary log book, record and interpret readings, lined notebook journal for tarot lovers. Independently Published.

Donati, S. (2006). Queen of Swords. Bantam.

Douglas, C. N. (1986). Six of Swords. Del Rey Books.

Durose-Rayner, J. (2017). Queen of Cups: Part 1. New Generation Publishing.

Eight of Cups Tarot card meanings. (2011, December 22). Biddy Tarot. https://www.biddytarot.com/tarot-card-meanings/minor-arcana/suit-of-cups/eight-of-cups/

Eight of Pentacles meaning, upright & reversed - guide. (n.d.). Mypandit.com. https://www.mypandit.com/amp/tarot/minor-arcana/suit-of-pentacles/eight-of-pentacles/

Eight of Pentacles Tarot card meanings. (2011, December 22). Biddy Tarot. https://www.biddytarot.com/tarot-card-meanings/minor-arcana/suit-of-pentacles/eight-of-pentacles/

Eight of swords meaning, upright & reversed – complete guide. (2021, March 16). MyPandit. https://www.mypandit.com/hindi/tarot/minor-arcana/suit-of-swords/eight-of-swords/

Eight of Swords Tarot card meanings. (2011, December 22). Biddy Tarot. https://www.biddytarot.com/tarot-card-meanings/minor-arcana/suit-of-swords/eight-of-swords/

Eight of wands meaning, love, upright & reversed - MyPandit. (n.d.). Mypandit.com. https://www.mypandit.com/amp/tarot/minor-arcana/suit-of-wands/eight-of-wands/

Eight of Wands Tarot card meanings. (2011, December 22). Biddy Tarot. https://www.biddytarot.com/tarot-card-meanings/minor-arcana/suit-of-wands/eight-of-wands/

emeraldlotus. (2018, September 18). Tarot Spread - Career Shift. Emerald Lotus Divination. https://www.emeraldlotusdivination.com/blog/2018/09/18/tarot-spread-career-shift

Emperor Tarot meaning, upright & reversed. (2021, April 1). MyPandit. https://www.mypandit.com/tarot/major-arcana/empror/

Empress Tarot meaning, love, feelings, upright & reversed – guide. (2021, April 5). MyPandit. https://www.mypandit.com/tarot/major-arcana/empress/

Esra. (2022, May 9). What Tarot Deck Should I Start With? The Best Tarot Decks For Beginners. Lamucidesign.Com. https://lamucidesign.com/what-tarot-deck-should-i-start-with-the-best-tarot-decks-for-beginners/

Esselmont, B. (2018, August 30). Dealing with Difficult Colleagues Tarot Card Spread. Biddy Tarot. https://www.biddytarot.com/difficult-colleagues-spread/

Esselmont, B. (2018, October 4). 9 Sure-Fire Ways to Select a Tarot Deck That's Right for You. Biddy Tarot. https://www.biddytarot.com/selecting-a-tarot-deck/

Five of cups meaning, upright & reversed. (2021, March 22). MyPandit. https://www.mypandit.com/tarot/minor-arcana/suit-of-cups/five-of-cups/

Five of Cups Tarot card meanings. (2011, December 22). Biddy Tarot. https://www.biddytarot.com/tarot-card-meanings/minor-arcana/suit-of-cups/five-of-cups/

Five of Cups. (n.d.). Astrotalk. https://astrotalk.com/tarot/five-of-cups

Five of pentacles meaning, upright & reverse – complete guide. (2021, April 1). MyPandit. https://www.mypandit.com/tarot/minor-arcana/suit-of-pentacles/five-of-pentacles/

Five of Pentacles Tarot card meanings. (2011, December 22). Biddy Tarot. https://www.biddytarot.com/tarot-card-meanings/minor-arcana/suit-of-pentacles/five-of-pentacles/

Five of swords meaning, upright & reversed – complete guide. (2021, March 22). MyPandit. https://www.mypandit.com/tarot/minor-arcana/suit-of-swords/five-of-swords/

Five of Swords Tarot card meanings. (2011, December 22). Biddy Tarot. https://www.biddytarot.com/tarot-card-meanings/minor-arcana/suit-of-swords/five-of-swords/

Five of wands meaning, upright & reversed – guide. (2021, March 18). MyPandit. https://www.mypandit.com/tarot/minor-arcana/suit-of-wands/five-of-wands/

Five of Wands Tarot card meanings. (2011, December 22). Biddy Tarot. https://www.biddytarot.com/tarot-card-meanings/minor-arcana/suit-of-wands/five-of-wands/

Fool Tarot meaning, love, feelings, upright & reversed – guide. (2021, March 16). MyPandit. https://www.mypandit.com/tarot/major-arcana/the-fool/

Four of Cups meaning – upright & reverse guide. (2021, March 22). MyPandit. https://www.mypandit.com/tarot/minor-arcana/suit-of-cups/four-of-cups/

Four of Cups Tarot card meanings. (2011, December 22). Biddy Tarot. https://www.biddytarot.com/tarot-card-meanings/minor-arcana/suit-of-cups/four-of-cups/

Four of Cups. (n.d.). Astrotalk. https://astrotalk.com/tarot/four-of-cups

Four of Pentacles Tarot card meaning, upright & reversed. (2021, March 31). MyPandit. https://www.mypandit.com/tarot/minor-arcana/suit-of-pentacles/four-of-pentacles/

Four of Pentacles Tarot card meanings. (2011, December 22). Biddy Tarot. https://www.biddytarot.com/tarot-card-meanings/minor-arcana/suit-of-pentacles/four-of-pentacles/

Four of swords meaning, upright & reverse – complete guide. (2021, March 24). MyPandit. https://www.mypandit.com/tarot/minor-arcana/suit-of-swords/four-of-swords/

Four of Swords Tarot card meanings. (2011, December 22). Biddy Tarot. https://www.biddytarot.com/tarot-card-meanings/minor-arcana/suit-of-swords/four-of-swords/

Four of Wands meaning, love, upright & reversed - MyPandit. (n.d.). Mypandit.com. https://www.mypandit.com/amp/tarot/minor-arcana/suit-of-wands/four-of-wands/

Four of Wands Tarot card meanings. (2011, December 22). Biddy Tarot. https://www.biddytarot.com/tarot-card-meanings/minor-arcana/suit-of-wands/four-of-wands/

Getting Answers About Your Job Hunt - A Job Tarot Spread. (2018, January 29). Labyrinthos. https://labyrinthos.co/blogs/learn-tarot-with-labyrinthos-academy/getting-answers-about-your-job-hunt-a-job-tarot-spread

Getts, Alex. 2022. "How to Connect with Your Tarot Cards." Intuitive Souls. June 30, 2022. https://www.intsouls.com/blog/how-to-connect-with-your-tarot-cards.

Girl), Kate (daily Tarot. 2012. "How to Connect with Your Tarot Deck in 3 Easy Steps." Daily Tarot Girl. Kate (Daily Tarot Girl). November 22, 2012. https://daily-tarot-girl.com/learn-tarot/how-connect-with-your-tarot-deck-3-easy-steps/.

Hastings, L. (2020). Seven of swords. Hobeck Books. https://astrotalk.com/tarot/seven-of-swords

High Priestess Tarot meaning, love, money, health, upright & reversed. (2021, March 12). MyPandit. https://www.mypandit.com/tarot/major-arcana/priestess/

How to Choose the Right Tarot Deck for You. (2020, January 20). Labyrinthos. https://labyrinthos.co/blogs/learn-tarot-with-labyrinthos-academy/how-to-choose-the-right-tarot-deck-for-you

How to create your own tarot spreads: A step by step guide and infographic. (2017, November 29). Labyrinthos. https://labyrinthos.co/blogs/learn-tarot-with-labyrinthos-academy/how-to-create-your-own-tarot-spreads-a-step-by-step-guide-and-infographic

https://www.biddytarot.com/

https://www.throughthephases.com/easy-three-card-Tarot-spreads/

Husband, T. (2016, April 8). Before Fortune-Telling: The History and Structure of Tarot Cards. The Metropolitan Museum of Art. https://www.metmuseum.org/blogs/in-season/2016/tarot

Jaiswal, R. (2022, October 9). How Many Tarot Cards In A Deck? The Island Now. https://theislandnow.com/how-many-tarot-cards-in-a-deck/

Judgement Tarot card meanings. (2011, December 22). Biddy Tarot. https://www.biddytarot.com/tarot-card-meanings/major-arcana/judgement/

Judgement Tarot Card Spread - A Tarot Spread for Reflection and Evaluation. (2021, March 2). Labyrinthos. https://labyrinthos.co/blogs/learn-tarot-with-labyrinthos-academy/judgement-tarot-card-spread

Judgement Tarot meaning, love, feelings, upright & reversed – guide. (2021, March 30). MyPandit. https://www.mypandit.com/tarot/major-arcana/judgement/

Judgement. (n.d.). Astrotalk. https://astrotalk.com/tarot/judgement

Jung And The Tarot. (n.d.). Meta-religion.com. https://www.meta-religion.com/Esoterism/Tarot/jung_and_the_tarot.htm

Justice Tarot card meanings. (2011, December 22). Biddy Tarot. https://www.biddytarot.com/tarot-card-meanings/major-arcana/justice/

Justice Tarot meaning, love, money, career, health, emotions, upright and reverse. (2021, July 21). MyPandit. https://www.mypandit.com/tarot/major-arcana/justice/

Justice. (n.d.). Astrotalk. https://astrotalk.com/tarot/justice

Kali, A. (2022, October 2). 10 things to know about tarot reading for marriage and relationships. Www.top10.com; Top10.com. https://www.top10.com/psychic-reading/tarot-readings-for-love

Kernick, S. (2018). The Hanged Man. Arrow Books.

Kim. 2018. "9 Ways to Connect and Bond with Your Tarot Cards." TarotLuv. September 19, 2018. https://tarotluv.com/blog/9-ways-to-connect-and-bond-with-your-tarot-cards/.

King of cups meaning, upright-reversed, feelings & guide! (2021, March 31). MyPandit. https://www.mypandit.com/tarot/royal-arcana/suit-of-cups/king-of-cups/

King of Cups Tarot card meanings. (2011, December 22). Biddy Tarot. https://www.biddytarot.com/tarot-card-meanings/minor-arcana/suit-of-cups/king-of-cups/

King of pentacles meaning, love, feelings, upright & reversed. (2022, November 3). MyPandit. https://www.mypandit.com/tarot/royal-arcana/suit-of-pentacles/king-of-pentacle

King of Pentacles Tarot card meanings. (2011, December 22). Biddy Tarot. https://www.biddytarot.com/tarot-card-meanings/minor-arcana/suit-of-pentacles/king-of-pentacles/

King of swords meaning, feelings, upright & reversed – complete guide. (2021, March 29). MyPandit. https://www.mypandit.com/tarot/royal-arcana/suit-of-swords/king-of-swords/

King of Swords Tarot card meanings. (2011, December 22). Biddy Tarot. https://www.biddytarot.com/tarot-card-meanings/minor-arcana/suit-of-swords/king-of-swords/

King of Wands Tarot card meanings. (2011, December 22). Biddy Tarot. https://www.biddytarot.com/tarot-card-meanings/minor-arcana/suit-of-wands/king-of-wands/

King of Wands Tarot meaning, love, upright & reversed – complete guide. (2021, March 30). MyPandit. https://www.mypandit.com/tarot/royal-arcana/suit-of-wands/king-of-wands/

Knight of cups meaning, love, feelings, upright & reversed - guide. (2021, March 29). MyPandit. https://www.mypandit.com/tarot/royal-arcana/suit-of-cups/knight-of-cups/

Knight of Cups Tarot card meanings. (2011, December 22). Biddy Tarot. https://www.biddytarot.com/tarot-card-meanings/minor-arcana/suit-of-cups/knight-of-cups/

Knight of pentacles meaning, love, upright & reversed - complete guide. (2021, March 25). MyPandit. https://www.mypandit.com/tarot/royal-arcana/suit-of-pentacles/knight-of-pentacles/

Knight of Pentacles Tarot card meanings. (2011, December 22). Biddy Tarot. https://www.biddytarot.com/tarot-card-meanings/minor-arcana/suit-of-pentacles/knight-of-pentacles/

Knight of swords meaning, love, upright & reversed - complete guide. (2021, March 30). MyPandit. https://www.mypandit.com/tarot/royal-arcana/suit-of-swords/knight-of-swords/

Knight of Swords Tarot card meanings. (2011, December 22). Biddy Tarot. https://www.biddytarot.com/tarot-card-meanings/minor-arcana/suit-of-swords/knight-of-swords/

Knight of wands meaning, love, feelings, upright & reversed. (2021, March 26). MyPandit. https://www.mypandit.com/tarot/royal-arcana/suit-of-wands/knight-of-wands/

Knight of Wands Tarot card meanings. (2011, December 22). Biddy Tarot. https://www.biddytarot.com/tarot-card-meanings/minor-arcana/suit-of-wands/knight-of-wands/

Leah. 2021. "8 Ways to Connect with Your Tarot Cards (or Reconnect with Your Deck)." Leah Vanderveldt. June 2, 2021. https://thenourishexchange.com/2021/06/8-ways-to-connect-with-your-tarot-cards-or-reconnect-with-your-deck/.

Love tarot card meaning, upright & reverse - complete guide. (2021, March 13). MyPandit. https://www.mypandit.com/tarot/major-arcana/lovers/

Luna Luna Staff. (2019, November 11). All The Ways You Can Use Tarot for Self-Care. Luna Luna Magazine. http://www.lunalunamagazine.com/dark/how-to-use-tarot-for-self-care

Macdonell, F. K. (2009). The fool's journey. iUniverse.com. http://www.learntarot.com/journey.htm

Magician Tarot meaning, love, feelings, upright & reversed - guide. (2021, April 5). MyPandit. https://www.mypandit.com/tarot/major-arcana/magician/

Making Tough Choices - A 5 Card Tarot Spread for Decision Making. (2018, September 11). Labyrinthos. https://labyrinthos.co/blogs/learn-tarot-with-labyrinthos-academy/making-tough-choices-a-5-card-tarot-spread-for-decision-making

Makino, E. B. (1994). Six of cups: A circle of stories. Earth Books.

Manifestor, M. (2020, October 28). How tarot cards work: The fool's journey & story of the major Arcana. Liz Roberta. https://lizroberta.com/2020/10/28/how-tarot-cards-work-the-fools-journey-story-of-the-major-arcana/

Milliner-Waddell, J. (2021, October 22). The Best Tarot and Oracle Decks, According to Tarot Readers and Astrologers. The Strategist. https://nymag.com/strategist/article/best-tarot-card-decks.html

Minor Arcana Tarot card meanings. (2011, December 18). Biddy Tarot. https://www.biddytarot.com/tarot-card-meanings/minor-arcana/

Moon tarot meaning, upright, reversed & guide. (2021, March 16). MyPandit. https://www.mypandit.com/tarot/major-arcana/moon/

Moore, J. K. (2007). Seven of cups. Wild Rose Press.

Munson, A. M. (2020). Five of pentacles: A bad granna mystery. Independently Published.

Nine of Cups meaning, love, upright & reversed. (2021, March 26). MyPandit. https://www.mypandit.com/tarot/minor-arcana/suit-of-cups/nine-of-cups/

Nine of Cups Tarot card meanings. (2011, December 22). Biddy Tarot. https://www.biddytarot.com/tarot-card-meanings/minor-arcana/suit-of-cups/nine-of-cups/

Nine of Cups. (n.d.). Astrotalk. https://astrotalk.com/tarot/nine-of-cups

Nine of pentacles meaning, love, feelings, upright & reversed. (2021, April 1). MyPandit. https://www.mypandit.com/tarot/minor-arcana/suit-of-pentacles/nine-of-pentacles/

Nine of Pentacles Tarot card meanings. (2011, December 22). Biddy Tarot. https://www.biddytarot.com/tarot-card-meanings/minor-arcana/suit-of-pentacles/nine-of-pentacles/

Nine of Swords meaning, feelings, upright & reversed. (2021, March 23). MyPandit. https://www.mypandit.com/tarot/minor-arcana/suit-of-swords/nine-of-swords/

Nine of Swords Tarot card meanings. (2011, December 22). Biddy Tarot. https://www.biddytarot.com/tarot-card-meanings/minor-arcana/suit-of-swords/nine-of-swords/

Page of cups meaning, love, feelings, upright & reversed – guide. (2021, March 26). MyPandit. https://www.mypandit.com/tarot/royal-arcana/suit-of-cups/page-of-cups/

Page of Cups Tarot card meanings. (2011, December 22). Biddy Tarot. https://www.biddytarot.com/tarot-card-meanings/minor-arcana/suit-of-cups/page-of-cups/

Page of pentacles meaning, love, feelings, upright & reversed – guide. (2021, April 5). MyPandit. https://www.mypandit.com/tarot/royal-arcana/suit-of-pentacles/page-of-pentacles/

Page of Pentacles Tarot card meanings. (2011, December 22). Biddy Tarot. https://www.biddytarot.com/tarot-card-meanings/minor-arcana/suit-of-pentacles/page-of-pentacles/

Page of swords meaning, feelings, upright & reversed – guide. (2021, March 30). MyPandit. https://www.mypandit.com/tarot/royal-arcana/suit-of-swords/page-of-swords/

Page of Swords Tarot card meanings. (2011, December 22). Biddy Tarot. https://www.biddytarot.com/tarot-card-meanings/minor-arcana/suit-of-swords/page-of-swords/

Page of wands meaning, love, feelings, upright & reversed – complete guide. (2021, March 26). MyPandit. https://www.mypandit.com/tarot/royal-arcana/suit-of-wands/page-of-wands/

Page of Wands Tarot card meanings. (2011, December 22). Biddy Tarot. https://www.biddytarot.com/tarot-card-meanings/minor-arcana/suit-of-wands/page-of-wands/

Queen of cups meaning, upright & reversed – complete guide. (2022, November 3). MyPandit. https://www.mypandit.com/tarot/royal-arcana/suit-of-cups/queen-of-cups-meaning-upright-reversed-complete-guide/

Queen of Cups Tarot card meanings. (2011, December 22). Biddy Tarot. https://www.biddytarot.com/tarot-card-meanings/minor-arcana/suit-of-cups/queen-of-cups/

Queen of pentacles meaning, love, upright & reversed – complete guide. (2021, March 31). MyPandit. https://www.mypandit.com/tarot/royal-arcana/suit-of-pentacles/queen-of-pentacles/

Queen of Pentacles Tarot card meanings. (2011, December 22). Biddy Tarot. https://www.biddytarot.com/tarot-card-meanings/minor-arcana/suit-of-pentacles/queen-of-pentacles/

Queen of swords meaning, love, upright & reversed – complete guide. (2021, March 19). MyPandit. https://www.mypandit.com/tarot/royal-arcana/suit-of-swords/queen-of-swords/

Queen of Swords Tarot card meanings. (2011, December 22). Biddy Tarot. https://www.biddytarot.com/tarot-card-meanings/minor-arcana/suit-of-swords/queen-of-swords/

Queen of wands meaning, upright & reversed - guide. (n.d.). Mypandit.com. https://www.mypandit.com/amp/tarot/royal-arcana/suit-of-wands/queen-of-wands/

Queen of Wands Tarot card meanings. (2011, December 22). Biddy Tarot. https://www.biddytarot.com/tarot-card-meanings/minor-arcana/suit-of-wands/queen-of-wands/

Rajatnayartopastrologer. (2017, July 7). Some amazing benefits of tarot card reading. Medium. https://medium.com/@rajatnayartopastrologer/some-amazing-benefits-of-tarot-card-reading-2131225a9b51

Reeder, B. S. (2015). Page of Swords. Createspace Independent Publishing Platform.

Roethle, S. C. (2017). Queen of Wands. Vulture's Eye Publications.

Rose, M. (2019). Tarot card meanings: The absolute beginner's guide to tarot card reading. Kontakt Digital.

Rosslee, J. (2022, July 31). Soulmate Tarot Spread explained: How to read this tarot spread? Tarot Technique. https://tarottechnique.com/tarot-spreads/soulmate-tarot-spread/

Sawyer, Eva. n.d. "Interviewing Your Tarot Deck." Tucumcari Tarot. https://www.tucumcaritarot.com/blog/nice-to-meet-you-insert-deck-name-here.

Seven of Cups meaning – upright & reversed. (2021, March 18). MyPandit. https://www.mypandit.com/tarot/minor-arcana/suit-of-cups/seven-of-cups/

Seven of Cups Tarot card meanings. (2011, December 22). Biddy Tarot. https://www.biddytarot.com/tarot-card-meanings/minor-arcana/suit-of-cups/seven-of-cups/

Seven of Pentacles meaning, love, feelings, upright & reversed – guide. (2021, March 26). MyPandit. https://www.mypandit.com/tarot/minor-arcana/suit-of-pentacles/seven-of-pentacles/

Seven of Pentacles Tarot card meanings. (2011, December 22). Biddy Tarot. https://www.biddytarot.com/tarot-card-meanings/minor-arcana/suit-of-pentacles/seven-of-pentacles/

Seven of Swords meaning, feelings, upright & reversed. (2021, March 23). MyPandit. https://www.mypandit.com/tarot/minor-arcana/suit-of-swords/seven-of-swords/

Seven of Swords Tarot card meanings. (2011, December 22). Biddy Tarot. https://www.biddytarot.com/tarot-card-meanings/minor-arcana/suit-of-swords/seven-of-swords/

Seven of Wands Tarot card meanings. (2011, December 22). Biddy Tarot. https://www.biddytarot.com/tarot-card-meanings/minor-arcana/suit-of-wands/seven-of-wands/

Seven of Wands tarot guide – upright & reversed. (2021, March 26). MyPandit. https://www.mypandit.com/tarot/minor-arcana/suit-of-wands/seven-of-wands/

Siday, L. (2022, September 5). Tree of Life Tarot Spread Guide. Tarot Technique. https://tarottechnique.com/tarot-spreads/tree-of-life-tarot-spread-guide/

Six of Cups Tarot card meanings. (2011, December 22). Biddy Tarot. https://www.biddytarot.com/tarot-card-meanings/minor-arcana/suit-of-cups/six-of-cups/

Six of Cups Tarot guide – upright & reversed. (2021, April 3). MyPandit. https://www.mypandit.com/tarot/minor-arcana/suit-of-cups/six-of-cups/

Six of pentacles meaning, love, feelings, upright & reversed – guide. (2021, March 31). MyPandit. https://www.mypandit.com/tarot/minor-arcana/suit-of-pentacles/six-of-pentacles/

Six of Pentacles Tarot card meanings. (2011, December 22). Biddy Tarot. https://www.biddytarot.com/tarot-card-meanings/minor-arcana/suit-of-pentacles/six-of-pentacles/

Six of swords meaning, love, upright & reversed – complete guide. (2021, March 26). MyPandit. https://www.mypandit.com/tarot/minor-arcana/suit-of-swords/six-of-swords/

Six of Swords Tarot card meanings. (2011, December 22). Biddy Tarot. https://www.biddytarot.com/tarot-card-meanings/minor-arcana/suit-of-swords/six-of-swords/

Six of wands meaning, love, upright & reverse – guide. (n.d.). Mypandit.com. https://www.mypandit.com/amp/tarot/minor-arcana/suit-of-wands/six-of-wands/

Six of Wands Tarot card meanings. (2011, December 22). Biddy Tarot. https://www.biddytarot.com/tarot-card-meanings/minor-arcana/suit-of-wands/six-of-wands/

Skibbins, D. (1957). Eight of swords. Griffin.

Stewart, G. C. (2017). The Hierophant. Andesite Press.

Strength Tarot card meanings. (2011, December 22). Biddy Tarot. https://www.biddytarot.com/tarot-card-meanings/major-arcana/strength/

Strength. (n.d.). Astrotalk. https://astrotalk.com/tarot/strength

Suit of Pentacles Tarot card meanings. (2013, March 10). Biddy Tarot. https://www.biddytarot.com/tarot-card-meanings/minor-arcana/suit-of-pentacles/

Suit of Swords Tarot card meanings. (2011, December 15). Biddy Tarot. https://www.biddytarot.com/tarot-card-meanings/minor-arcana/suit-of-swords/

Suit of Wands Tarot card meanings. (2011, December 15). Biddy Tarot. https://www.biddytarot.com/tarot-card-meanings/minor-arcana/suit-of-wands/

Tarot Card Reading. (n.d.). Astrotalk. https://astrotalk.com/tarot

Tarot de Marseille by Vieux Monde Express. (n.d.). Buyolympia. https://buyolympia.com/Item/tarot-de-marseille-deck

Tarot, M. (2013, March 26). The Soul Activation Spread for Spiritual Growth. Mister Tarot. https://www.mistertarot.com/tarot-spirituality/

Tempera, J. (2022, September 22). How To Do Beginner Tarot Card Spreads, According To Experts. Women's Health. https://www.womenshealthmag.com/life/a41319340/beginner-tarot-spreads/

Temperance Tarot card meanings. (2011, December 22). Biddy Tarot. https://www.biddytarot.com/tarot-card-meanings/major-arcana/temperance/

Temperance Tarot guide – meaning, upright, reversed & love. (2021, March 25). MyPandit. https://www.mypandit.com/tarot/major-arcana/temperance/

Temperance. (n.d.). Astrotalk. https://astrotalk.com/tarot/temperance

Ten of Cups Tarot card meanings. (2011, December 22). Biddy Tarot. https://www.biddytarot.com/tarot-card-meanings/minor-arcana/suit-of-cups/ten-of-cups/

Ten of Cups. (n.d.). Astrotalk. https://astrotalk.com/tarot/ten-of-cups

Ten of Pentacles meaning, upright & reversed - guide. (n.d.). Mypandit.com. https://www.mypandit.com/amp/tarot/minor-arcana/suit-of-pentacles/ten-of-pentacles

Ten of Pentacles Tarot card meanings. (2011, December 22). Biddy Tarot. https://www.biddytarot.com/tarot-card-meanings/minor-arcana/suit-of-pentacles/ten-of-pentacles

Ten of Swords Tarot card meaning, love, feelings, upright & reversed. (2021, March 30). MyPandit. https://www.mypandit.com/tarot/minor-arcana/suit-of-swords/ten-of-swords/

Ten of Swords Tarot card meanings. (2011, December 22). Biddy Tarot. https://www.biddytarot.com/tarot-card-meanings/minor-arcana/suit-of-swords/ten-of-swords/

Ten of wands meaning, upright & reversed - guide. (2021, March 19). MyPandit. https://www.mypandit.com/tarot/minor-arcana/suit-of-wands/ten-of-wands/

Ten of Wands Tarot card meanings. (2011, December 22). Biddy Tarot. https://www.biddytarot.com/tarot-card-meanings/minor-arcana/suit-of-wands/ten-of-wands/

The Chariot Tarot card meanings. (2011, December 22). Biddy Tarot. https://www.biddytarot.com/tarot-card-meanings/major-arcana/chariot/

The Chariot. (n.d.). Astrotalk. https://astrotalk.com/tarot/the-chariot

The Devil Tarot card meanings. (2011, December 22). Biddy Tarot. https://www.biddytarot.com/tarot-card-meanings/major-arcana/devil/

The Devil. (n.d.). Astrotalk. https://astrotalk.com/tarot/the-devil

The Emperor Tarot card meanings. (2011, December 22). Biddy Tarot. https://www.biddytarot.com/tarot-card-meanings/major-arcana/emperor/

The Emperor Tarot Card Spread - A Tarot Spread for Claiming Personal Power. (2021, February 5). Labyrinthos. https://labyrinthos.co/blogs/learn-tarot-with-labyrinthos-academy/the-emperor-tarot-card-spread

The emperor. (n.d.). Astrotalk. https://astrotalk.com/tarot/the-emperor

The Empress Tarot card meanings. (2011, December 22). Biddy Tarot. https://www.biddytarot.com/tarot-card-meanings/major-arcana/empress/

The Empress. (n.d.). Astrotalk. https://astrotalk.com/tarot/the-empress

The Fool -. (2011, October 21). Tarot Elements. https://tarotelements.com/tarot-card-meanings/major-arcana/fool/

The Fool Tarot card meanings. (2011, December 23). Biddy Tarot. https://www.biddytarot.com/tarot-card-meanings/major-arcana/fool/

The Hanged Man Tarot card meaning, feelings, upright & reversed. (2021, April 1). MyPandit. https://www.mypandit.com/tarot/major-arcana/hanged-man/

The Hanged Man Tarot card meanings. (2011, December 22). Biddy Tarot. https://www.biddytarot.com/tarot-card-meanings/major-arcana/hanged-man/

The Hermit Tarot card meanings. (2011, December 22). Biddy Tarot. https://www.biddytarot.com/tarot-card-meanings/major-arcana/hermit/

The Hermit tarot guide - upright & reverse guide. (2021, March 22). MyPandit. https://www.mypandit.com/tarot/major-arcana/hermit/

The Hermit. (n.d.). Astrotalk. https://astrotalk.com/tarot/the-hermit

The Hierophant Tarot card meanings. (2011, December 22). Biddy Tarot. https://www.biddytarot.com/tarot-card-meanings/major-arcana/hierophant/

The High Priestess meaning - major Arcana tarot card meanings. (2017, March 6). Labyrinthos. https://labyrinthos.co/blogs/tarot-card-meanings-list/the-high-priestess-meaning-major-arcana-tarot-card-meanings

The High Priestess Tarot card meanings. (2011, December 22). Biddy Tarot. https://www.biddytarot.com/tarot-card-meanings/major-arcana/high-priestess/

The High Priestess. (n.d.). Astrotalk. https://astrotalk.com/tarot/the-high-priestess

The Lovers. (n.d.). Astrotalk. https://astrotalk.com/tarot/the-lovers

The magician -. (2011, October 21). Tarot Elements. https://tarotelements.com/tarot-card-meanings/major-arcana/magician/

The Magician meaning - major Arcana tarot card meanings. (2017, March 6). Labyrinthos. https://labyrinthos.co/blogs/tarot-card-meanings-list/the-magician-meaning-major-arcana-tarot-card-meanings

The Magician Tarot card meanings. (2011, December 22). Biddy Tarot. https://www.biddytarot.com/tarot-card-meanings/major-arcana/magician/

the magus. (n.d.). Tumblr. https://sylvaetria.tumblr.com/post/164609909472/flower-of-life-tarot-spread-current-energies

The Major Arcana Tarot card meanings. (2017, February 2). Tarot.com. https://www.tarot.com/tarot/cards/major-arcana

The Minor Arcana tarot cards. (2016, February 19). Tarot.com. https://www.tarot.com/tarot/cards/minor-arcana

The Moon Tarot card meanings. (2011, December 22). Biddy Tarot. https://www.biddytarot.com/tarot-card-meanings/major-arcana/moon/

The moon. (n.d.). Astrotalk. https://astrotalk.com/tarot/the-moon

The Star Tarot card meanings. (2011, December 22). Biddy Tarot. https://www.biddytarot.com/tarot-card-meanings/major-arcana/star/

The Strength tarot guide – upright & reversed. (2021, April 6). MyPandit. https://www.mypandit.com/tarot/major-arcana/strength/

The suit of cups tarot card meanings. (2020, January 28). Labyrinthos. https://labyrinthos.co/blogs/tarot-card-meanings-list/the-suit-of-cups-tarot-card-meanings

The suit of pentacles tarot card meanings. (2020, January 28). Labyrinthos. https://labyrinthos.co/blogs/tarot-card-meanings-list/the-suit-of-pentacles-tarot-card-meanings

The suit of swords tarot card meanings. (2020, January 28). Labyrinthos. https://labyrinthos.co/blogs/tarot-card-meanings-list/the-suit-of-swords-tarot-card-meanings

The Sun Tarot card meaning – upright & reverse guide. (2021, March 18). MyPandit. https://www.mypandit.com/tarot/major-arcana/sun/

The Sun Tarot card meanings. (2011, December 22). Biddy Tarot. https://www.biddytarot.com/tarot-card-meanings/major-arcana/sun/

The Sun. (n.d.). Astrotalk. https://astrotalk.com/tarot/the-sun

The three of Pentacles Tarot guide – upright & reversed. (2021, April 5). MyPandit. https://www.mypandit.com/tarot/minor-arcana/suit-of-pentacles/three-of-pentacles/

The Three of Swords Tarot guide – upright & reversed. (2021, March 16). MyPandit. https://www.mypandit.com/tarot/minor-arcana/suit-of-swords/three-of-swords/

The Tower Tarot card meanings. (2011, December 22). Biddy Tarot. https://www.biddytarot.com/tarot-card-meanings/major-arcana/tower/

The tower. (n.d.). Astrotalk. https://astrotalk.com/tarot/the-tower

The World Tarot card meanings. (2011, December 22). Biddy Tarot. https://www.biddytarot.com/tarot-card-meanings/major-arcana/world/

The World Tarot meaning – upright & reversed. (2021, March 25). MyPandit. https://www.mypandit.com/tarot/major-arcana/world/

The World. (n.d.). Astrotalk. https://astrotalk.com/tarot/the-world

Thoth Tarot 101: Let This Amazing Deck Guide Your Life. (2021, September 16). A Little Spark of Joy. https://www.alittlesparkofjoy.com/thoth-tarot/

Three Career Tarot Spreads for Finding Your Path and Calling. (2016, December 1). Labyrinthos. https://labyrinthos.co/blogs/learn-tarot-with-labyrinthos-academy/three-career-tarot-spreads-for-finding-your-path-and-calling

Three of Cups meaning, love, upright and reversed – complete guide. (2021, March 16). MyPandit. https://www.mypandit.com/tarot/minor-arcana/suit-of-cups/three-of-cups/

Three of Cups Tarot card meanings. (2011, December 22). Biddy Tarot. https://www.biddytarot.com/tarot-card-meanings/minor-arcana/suit-of-cups/three-of-cups/

Three of Cups. (n.d.). Astrotalk. https://astrotalk.com/tarot/three-of-cups

Three of Pentacles Tarot card meanings. (2011, December 22). Biddy Tarot. https://www.biddytarot.com/tarot-card-meanings/minor-arcana/suit-of-pentacles/three-of-pentacles/

Three of wands meaning, love, feelings, upright & reversed – guide. (2021, May 5). MyPandit. https://www.mypandit.com/tarot/minor-arcana/suit-of-wands/three-of-wands/

Three of Wands Tarot card meanings. (2011, December 22). Biddy Tarot. https://www.biddytarot.com/tarot-card-meanings/minor-arcana/suit-of-wands/three-of-wands/

Tramble, Rashunda. 2021. "10 Ways to Connect with Your New Tarot Deck —." Stay Woke Tarot. July 13, 2021. https://www.staywoketarot.com/blog/10-ways-to-connect-with-your-new-tarot-deck/.

TrulyLiving. 2018. "How to Attune a Deck of Cards for Divination." Truly Living with Lisa Rose | Soul Coach & Reiki. February 12, 2018. https://www.trulyliving.net/how-to-attune-a-deck-of-cards-for-divination/.

Two of cups meaning, upright & reversed – complete guide. (2021, March 23). MyPandit. https://www.mypandit.com/tarot/minor-arcana/suit-of-cups/two-of-cups/

Two of Cups Tarot card meanings. (2011, December 22). Biddy Tarot. https://www.biddytarot.com/tarot-card-meanings/minor-arcana/suit-of-cups/two-of-cups/

Two of Cups. (n.d.). Astrotalk. https://astrotalk.com/tarot/two-of-cups

Two of Pentacles Tarot card meanings. (2011, December 22). Biddy Tarot. https://www.biddytarot.com/tarot-card-meanings/minor-arcana/suit-of-pentacles/two-of-pentacles/

Two of Pentacles. (2021, March 16). MyPandit. https://www.mypandit.com/hindi/tarot/minor-arcana/suit-of-pentacles/two-of-pentacles/

Two of swords meaning, upright & reverse - complete guide. (2021, March 23). MyPandit. https://www.mypandit.com/tarot/minor-arcana/suit-of-swords/two-of-swords/

Two of Swords Tarot card meanings. (2011, December 22). Biddy Tarot. https://www.biddytarot.com/tarot-card-meanings/minor-arcana/suit-of-swords/two-of-swords/

Two of Swords. (n.d.). Astrotalk. https://astrotalk.com/tarot/two-of-swords

Two of Wands Tarot card meanings. (2011, December 22). Biddy Tarot. https://www.biddytarot.com/tarot-card-meanings/minor-arcana/suit-of-wands/two-of-wands/

Two of Wands tarot guide - upright & reversed. (2021, March 23). MyPandit. https://www.mypandit.com/tarot/minor-arcana/suit-of-wands/two-of-wands/

What does The High Priestess Tarot card mean? (2019, August 29).

What does The Magician Tarot card mean? (2019, August 29).

Wheel of Fortune Tarot card meanings. (2011, December 22). Biddy Tarot. https://www.biddytarot.com/tarot-card-meanings/major-arcana/wheel-of-fortune/

Wheel of Fortune tarot meaning, love, upright & reversed - complete guide. (2021, March 26). MyPandit. https://www.mypandit.com/tarot/major-arcana/wheel-of-fortune/

Wheels of fortune. (2006). New Scientist (1971), 191(2566), 85. https://doi.org/10.1016/s0262-4079(06)60311-4

Wigington, P. (n.d.). A Brief History of Tarot. Learn Religions. https://www.learnreligions.com/a-brief-history-of-tarot-2562770

Wille. (2020, July 31). Ten of Cups tarot card meaning. A Little Spark of Joy. https://www.alittlesparkofjoy.com/ten-of-cups-tarot-card-meanings/

Wille. (2021, February 5). 9 easy tarot Love spreads to spread the Love. A Little Spark of Joy. https://www.alittlesparkofjoy.com/tarot-love-spreads/

Wille. (2021, November 16). Four of Swords tarot card meaning: Love, health, money & more. A Little Spark of Joy. https://www.alittlesparkofjoy.com/four-of-swords-tarot-card-meaning/

Yotka, S. (2016, August 4). Tarot 101: A Beginner's Guide. Vogue. https://www.vogue.com/article/tarot-101-beginner-guide-how-to-small-spells

# Image Sources

1 Image by Mira Cosic, Astrologer from Pixabay https://pixabay.com/photos/tarot-cards-magic-fortune-telling-991041/

2 Roberto Viesi, CC BY-SA 4.0 <https://creativecommons.org/licenses/by-sa/4.0>, via Wikimedia Commons https://commons.wikimedia.org/wiki/File:The_Major_Arcana_by_Roberto_Viesi.jpg

3 Image by Virgo Gem from Pixabay https://pixabay.com/illustrations/el-tonto-tarot-tarjeta-magia-6016940/

4 Image by Virgo Gem from Pixabay https://pixabay.com/illustrations/el-mago-cartas-de-tarot-tarot-mago-6103696/

5 Image by Virgo Gem from Pixabay https://pixabay.com/illustrations/tarot-tarot-cards-magic-fortune-6246912/

6 Image by Virgo Gem from Pixabay https://pixabay.com/illustrations/emperatriz-carta-de-tarot-s%c3%admbolo-6016923/

7 Image by Virgo Gem from Pixabay https://pixabay.com/illustrations/tarot-cartas-de-tarot-el-emperador-6129696/

8 Image by Virgo Gem from Pixabay https://pixabay.com/illustrations/el-hierofante-tarot-tarjeta-magia-6016942/

9 Image by Virgo Gem from Pixabay https://pixabay.com/illustrations/cartas-de-tarot-tarot-amantes-magia-6103697/

10 Image by Virgo Gem from Pixabay https://pixabay.com/illustrations/carruaje-tarot-tarjeta-magia-6016921/

11 Image by Virgo Gem from Pixabay https://pixabay.com/illustrations/tarot-cartas-de-tarot-fuerza-6129685/

12 Image by Virgo Gem from Pixabay https://pixabay.com/illustrations/ermita%c3%b1o-tarot-tarjeta-magia-6016941/

13 Image by Virgo Gem from Pixabay https://pixabay.com/illustrations/tarot-cartas-de-tarot-6129686/

14 Image by Virgo Gem from Pixabay https://pixabay.com/illustrations/tarot-cartas-de-tarot-justicia-6129675/

15 Image by Virgo Gem from Pixabay https://pixabay.com/illustrations/tarot-cartas-de-tarot-justicia-6129675/

16 Image by Virgo Gem from Pixabay https://pixabay.com/illustrations/cartas-de-tarot-tarot-muerte-magia-6103718/

17 Image by Virgo Gem from Pixabay https://pixabay.com/illustrations/templanza-tarot-tarjeta-magia-6016917/

18 https://freesvg.org/devil-tarot-card

19 Image by Virgo Gem from Pixabay https://pixabay.com/illustrations/tarot-cards-tarot-tower-magic-6103701/

20 Image by Virgo Gem from Pixabay https://pixabay.com/illustrations/tarot-cards-tarot-star-magic-cards-6103699/

21 Image by Virgo Gem from Pixabay https://pixabay.com/illustrations/tarot-cards-tarot-moon-magic-cards-6103698/

22 Image by Virgo Gem from Pixabay https://pixabay.com/illustrations/tarot-cards-tarot-sun-magic-cards-6103700/

23 Image by Virgo Gem from Pixabay https://pixabay.com/illustrations/tarot-tarot-cards-judgement-cards-6129676/

24 Image by Virgo Gem from Pixabay https://pixabay.com/illustrations/tarot-cards-tarot-world-magic-6103702/

25 Photo by Viva Luna Studios on Unsplash https://unsplash.com/photos/king-of-diamonds-playing-card-0-7oZdFHf-I

26 Photo by petr sidorov on Unsplash https://unsplash.com/photos/D3SzBCAeMhQ

27 Photo by Kayla Maurais on Unsplash https://unsplash.com/photos/1t2Kjo4Smpc

28 carbonnyc, Attribution 2.0 Generic, CC BY 2.0, <https://creativecommons.org/licenses/by/2.0/deed.en> https://www.flickr.com/photos/carbonnyc/5101424798

www.ingramcontent.com/pod-product-compliance
Lightning Source LLC
Chambersburg PA
CBHW051851160426
43209CB00006B/1256